Where Five Roa

A History of Wragby, Lincolnshire

Supported by
The National Lottery®
through Awards for All

AWARDS
FOR ALL

ISBN 978-0-9557768-0-9

Published by Wragby Heritage Group
Compiled and Edited by Juliet Smith
Sub-Editor: Karen Nash

Printed by Cupit Print, Horncastle, Lincolnshire

Cover Picture
Market Place, Wragby from a painting c.1820
Commissioned by John H. Edwards in 1984
Painted by Lincoln Artist David J. Dunthorne

Frontispiece
All Saints Church, Wragby, Lincolnshire

INTRODUCTION

Many people only know Wragby as a convenient comfort stop on their journeys to and from the coast, via Lincoln. However, on closer inspection, Wragby has a lot more to offer the discerning traveller.

It is a place of hidden depths and history. For instance, did you know that Wragby has a mention in the Domesday Book and that its history goes even further back than that? Were you aware that Henry III, Charles II and the Duke of Buckingham played a part in Wragby's history? Did you know that the Lincolnshire Museum holds some artefacts found in Wragby?

Have we whetted your appetite yet? If so then read on. The purpose of this book is to make people aware that Wragby is more than it appears, more than just a stopping off place. As you delve further you will learn more about the people of Wragby, the highs and lows and the decline and rise of the population and its industry. Wragby has changed much over the years. It may not look much but do we have a history.

This book comes with a Heritage Trail leaflet. After reading the book you might like to take a walk around Wragby and actually see some of the places mentioned.

The Old Vicarage

Forewords

Wragby Heritage Group was formed in 2002 and one of their aims was the challenging task of preparing a book about the history of Wragby - a history that covers every century of the preceding thousand years.

After many years of thought it is only recently that the research, collating and editing has been undertaken. The end result is this fine volume.

In these pages are vivid accounts of notable historical events, memorable local figures and fascinating buildings and places. But there is also evidence of a strong community life that has been at the very heart of Wragby down the years.

Thanks must go to all those who helped in so many ways to make this book possible. For it is both a splendid record of the past, and also a source of inspiration and encouragement for us in this generation, as we journey forward together into the next chapter in the fascinating history of our community.

Rev. Mark Holden
Vicar of Wragby

We are indebted to everyone who has given time, talent and resources to produce this history.

We can already hear folk commenting "Oh I remember her/ him weren't they related to that family who lived on Louth Road?" or "That house, estate or road is so completely different now and didn't he/she work just over there?"

As we read, memories of faces and situations will come flooding back and new information will be stumbled across. We will perhaps catch a sense that 'time' is a relentless part of our lives and within this space from 'birth to death' contributions to our community, by individuals and groups have left their mark.

I suspect the dominant theme will be of how the physical shape and structure of Wragby has changed dramatically, within everyone's living memory. The contributors to this anthology recognise that the documentation of this change and how we all interpret it will inform how Wragby develops and moves forward into the twenty first century.

Why write a history? There are many reasons beyond nostalgia, one being, to make sure mistakes are not repeated but equally that opportunities are not missed to ensure that Wragby remains a cohesive and functioning community where people are welcomed and appreciated!

Thank you to all who have brought this project to a successful completion.

Rev Canon Alan J Robson
(Methodist Minister- Ecumenical Canon Lincoln Cathedral
Lincolnshire Agricultural Chaplain 1999-)

Contents

Acknowledgements

The reasons for producing this book are manifold. The Heritage Group wanted to record the history of Wragby throughout its long existence; the unique experience of having been owned by one family for over 200 years and the effect this had on its development. We also wanted to preserve the memories of some of the older residents for the future, and to record some of the events which gave Wragby its character.

In publishing this book we hope that it will give residents, old and new, a sense of the place in which they live. More importantly, we hope it will portray a sense of history and pride in the younger members of the community, within whose hands the future of Wragby lies.

Obviously we could not do this alone, and many people and organisations have assisted us in the production of this book. It is impossible to mention all by name and we apologise to those who do not get a personal mention, but we think that the following deserve a special mention.

As Chairman I would personally like to thank all the members, past and present, of the Wragby Heritage Group, who conceived the idea and who have researched and correlated the material in the book.

As a group we would like to say thank you to all the local people, businesses and organisations, who shared their memories, their mementoes and their records with us. Thanks also to those, whose families lived and worked here in the past, who have provided invaluable information. A special mention also to Anglian Water and Jack Evans for technical details.

A big thank you is due to John Edwards for putting his vast collection of local photographs and documents at our disposal and also to those people who have contributed to his collection. Without these our work would not have been possible.

Great use has been made of the Lincolnshire Archives, the Lincolnshire Library Service and the Historic Buildings and Monuments Department of Lincolnshire County Council, and we would like to thank them for their time and efforts in helping us to carry out our research.

Throughout the book you will find anecdotes of daily life as written by the school children of 1964 in the 'Wragby Sun'. We would like to thank them also.

Finally we have to thank 'Awards for All' for their generous grant, which has enabled us to bring our ideas into fruition. We would also like to mention that the proceeds from this book will be put towards obtaining pictorial signs for the major roads into Wragby, in conjunction with the Parish Council.

To those others who contributed their time and knowledge we would like to say a big thank you.

We hope that you enjoy this book.

Victor Nash

PROFILE

Wragby is a small market town in East Lindsey, placed on the spring line between the chalk and limestone ridges of the Lincolnshire Edge and the Lincolnshire Wolds. It lies on the crossing of five roads to Lincoln, Skegness, Louth, Market Rasen and Bardney with the Market Place at the junction.

It is almost self-sufficient in that it has a Town Hall, Post Office, Newsagent, Butcher, Grocery Store, Greengrocer, Hairdressers, a Fish and Chip Shop and various other businesses including two Public Houses, a Licensed Club and a Licensed Restaurant. Wragby also has an Anglican Church, a Methodist Church, a Sports Hall, Swimming Pool, Doctors' Surgery and Resource Centre, which now has library facilities. Until recently it also had a mobile bank, but this was withdrawn by HSBC as being uneconomical. The mobile library ceased when the Resource Centre opened its library services.

The earliest known history of the area goes back to the Coritani, who were a loose confederation of tribes whose economy was based primarily on cattle, and they settled the area from Leicestershire up to North Yorkshire and across to Nottinghamshire. From archaeological finds it is believed that they inhabited the area from about 50 to 1 BC before joining with other tribes to form the Corieltauvi. It is thought that the Corieltauvi tribe was formed shortly before the Roman Conquest and, as they did not offer much resistance to the Romans, was quickly turned into an administrative district, much like a county council of today.

It is well documented elsewhere what benefits the Romans brought to the area and that Lincoln was a Roman Metropolis and Horncastle an established Roman town. It is also known that the Roman Road from Lincoln to Burgh-le-Marsh (with its subsequent turn off for Horncastle) passed within a mile of Wragby Centre. Therefore it is possible that there might have been some form of settlement or staging post or even just a watering hole here, where the Romans of the day stopped and rested before continuing their journey. At least we like to think so and it would make sense of the fact that the Vikings established the centre of the Wraggoe Wapentake here.

When the Romans left the area in the 5th century it was reportedly deserted until incoming groups of Angles settled heavily in the region. The Anglian Kingdom of Lindsey was then established until it was absorbed by Mercia in the 8th century. This was the time of the Vikings! Lincolnshire was within the part of Mercia that was ceded to the Viking Army in 874 AD following the defeat of the Mercian King, Burgred, at Repton. One result of this defeat was that scores of Scandinavians settled in the areas controlled by the Danes, thus Danelaw was born.

In the 10th century, Lincoln became the head of the new shire of Lincolnshire. Wragby was the centre of the Wraggoe Wapentake, an administrative area under Danelaw, which is how much of Northern England was divided. The Wraggoe Wapentake court would have met regularly throughout the year, possibly on higher ground than Wragby stands at present, as the ending of the word Wraggoe means 'mound'. There are many legacies left us by the Scandinavians especially in place names.

The name Wragby is either taken from the Scandinavian name of '*Wraggi*' with the addition of 'by' meaning homestead or it is a derivation of the Old Norse term for wolf, which is '*vargr*'. This word, in the ancient Saxon of the Heliand, is *Warag*, which is identical to the spelling in the Domesday Book.

The English recaptured Lincolnshire around 920 AD but it was the defeat of Eric Bloodaxe in the middle of the 10th century that enabled the English finally to establish control. Having said that, it would appear that in 1013 Sweyn of Denmark landed at Gainsborough. In preparation for an assault of England and, having received the submission of Northumbria and Lindsey, he marched south leaving the area in control of his son, Cnut. Sweyn was eventually recognised as King of England but died in 1014 leaving his son as king.

After William the Conqueror defeated Harold II at Hastings in 1066 and established himself as King of England, he ordered a survey to be done of all England. It is not known when the survey began but it is generally agreed that it was completed in 1086 and was to be known as the Domesday Book (so named, we believe, because of the finality of the judgements on the value, tenure and services of lands described). The survey of Lincolnshire is thought to have been carried out in 1085 and at that time Wragby or Waragebi comprised two manors and subsequently two entries in the Domesday Book. Countess Gudeta owned the Principal manor which was subsequently given to Ernies de Buron; the second was owned by Godevert and given to Waldin the Engineer. Both entries are illustrated below.

Unfortunately, there are some discrepancies in the translation of the entry for Ernies de Buron. Although the name Gudeta appears in the original, some translate this to mean Countess Judith, niece of William the Conqueror and some have it that Gudeta was sister to Sweyn, King of Denmark and England, wife of Earl Godwin and mother of Earl Harold. However, this raises the question that if it was Countess Judith, why did William remove her lands in favour of Ernies de Buron? According to historical entries elsewhere, the mother of Earl Harold and wife of Godwin was Gytha and no entry for Sweyn of Denmark has him listed with a sister, or anyone else, called Gudeta. So that leaves us with a dilemma which may or may not, ever be resolved.

What is clear is the standing of each manor:
Countess Gudeta had 6½ bovates of land taxable and land for 12 oxen. Ernies had 1 plough and 10 villagers with 1½ ploughs. There was a church with a priest; ½ a mill worth 12d yearly; a meadow of 24 acres; a wood containing pasturage for cattle 4 furlongs wide and 4 furlongs long; underwood 5 furlongs long and 5 furlongs wide. The annual value in King Edward's time was £14 and the value now £10 with taxes of £10.

Godevert had 5½ bovates of land taxable and land for 2 ploughs. Waldin had 1 plough and 3 freemen with 2 bovates of this land; 4 villagers and 5 smallholders with 1½ ploughs; a mill site; 16 acres of meadow and 240 acres of woodland containing pasturage in places. The annual value in King Edward's time was 30s and the value now 35s with taxes of 5s.

To help envisage the size of each manor these definitions may prove useful:
Bovate - the area of land that 1 ox can plough in one year i.e., ⅛ of 120 acres = 15 acres.
Plough - A team of 8 oxen including the plough itself.
Villager - A member of the peasant class with most land.

The manor of Ernies de Buron, which included the church, was the largest of the manors and the centre of a substantial estate. The remains of the manor site can be seen in the fields at the end of Cemetery Road on the right hand side, commonly known as the mounds and Rout Yard. Below is an aerial view taken by Lincolnshire County Council which shows the outline of the moated islands of the manor, the old church and cemetery and also the old fish ponds.

Since then the Manor of Wragby has passed through various hands. The largest portion was owned by the Fitz-Payne family in the 12th century and formed part of the Barony of Trusbut. It then passed to the Dukes of Rutland - The Roos family - then the Manners family until the marriage of Katherine Manners, Baroness of Roos, with George Villiers, the Duke of Buckingham.

The smaller portion had passed from Waldin the Engineer to the Bishop of Lincoln and in the 15th century it passed to the Sandons of Ashby by Partney.

As far back as 1221, in the reign of Henry III, William de Roos obtained permission to hold a weekly Thursday market at the manor. It appears that this was applied for and granted yearly 'until the King became of age' and the Sheriff of Lincolnshire was duly notified. In 1223 the day of the market was changed to a Wednesday and in 1227 the Sheriff of Lincolnshire was ordered to exempt the market from the general prohibition of markets and fairs raised during the minority of King Henry III. The Wednesday market was still being held in 1384.

In view of this, it is surprising that in 1669 the Duke of Buckingham, George Villiers, felt it necessary to obtain a Charter from King Charles II, to hold a market on Thursday of every week throughout the year and also three new fairs to be held on 24th February, 18th September and 8th October annually. A copy of the Charter is shown below and on the following pages.

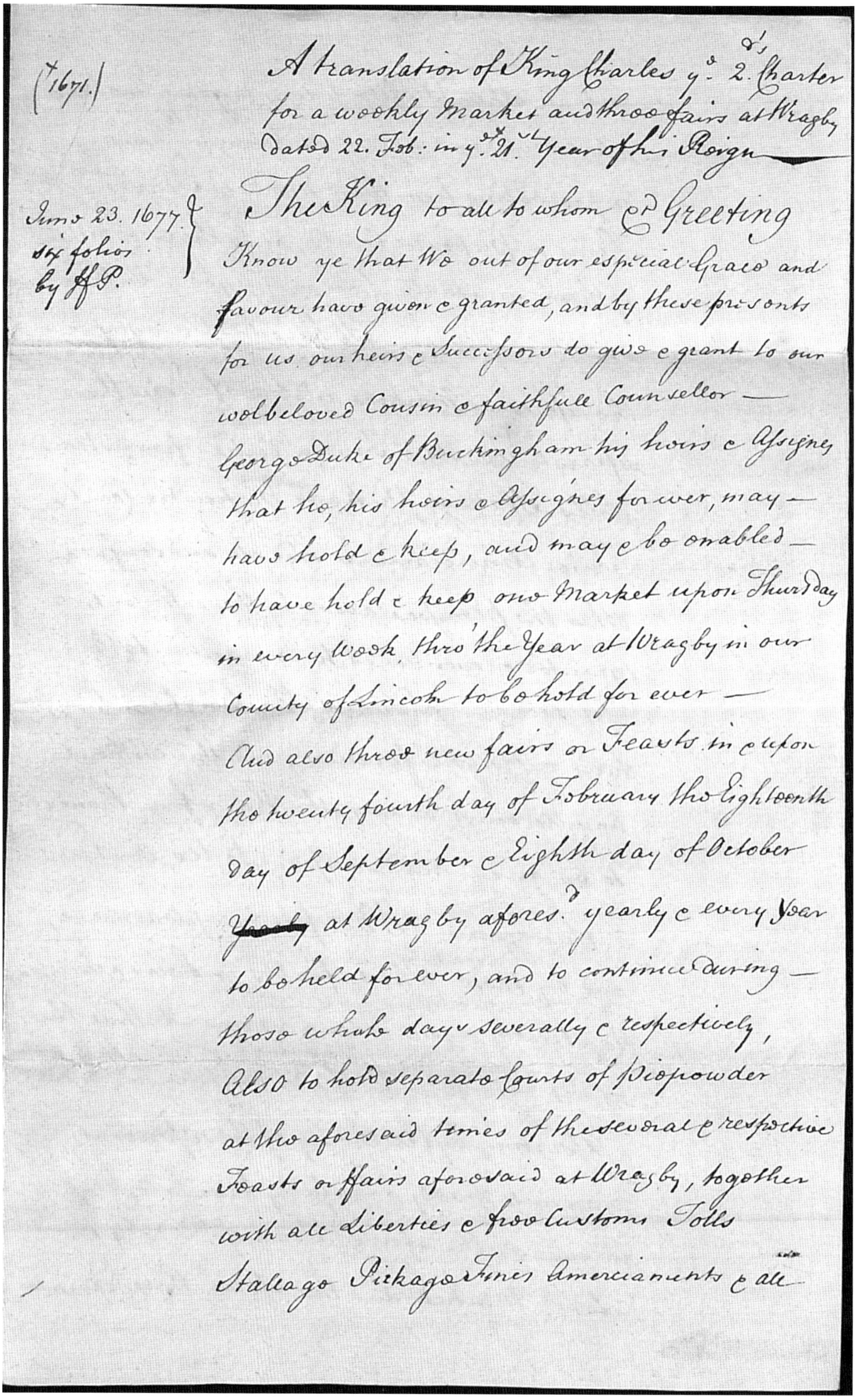

(1671.)

June 23. 1677.
six folios
by H.P.

A translation of King Charles ye 2. Charter
for a weekly Market and three fairs at Wragby
Dated 22. Feb: in ye 21st Year of his Reign

The King to all to whom &c Greeting
Know ye that We out of our especial Grace and
favour have given & granted, and by these presents
for us, our heirs & Successors do give & grant to our
welbeloved Cousin & faithfull Counsellor —
George Duke of Buckingham his heirs & Assignes
that he, his heirs & Assignes for ever, may —
have hold & keep, and may & be enabled —
to have hold & keep, one Market upon Thursday
in every Week, thro' the Year at Wragby in our
County of Lincoln to be hold for ever —
And also three new fairs or Feasts in & upon
the twenty fourth day of February the Eighteenth
Day of September & Eighth day of October
Yearly at Wragby aforesd yearly & every Year
to be held for ever, and to continue during —
those whole days severally & respectively,
Also to hold separate Courts of Piepowder
at the aforesaid times of the several & respective
Feasts or fairs aforesaid at Wragby, together
with all Liberties & free Customs Tolls
Stallage Pickage Fines Amerciaments & all

10

and all other Profits Advantages Emoluments
whatsoever in any respect belonging to, arising
or proceeding from, those Markets Feasts or
Fairs & Piepowder Courts, or to them or either
of them, or usually had or enjoyed with them
or either of them — To have hold & enjoy —
the aforesaid Markets and the aforesaid three
separate Feasts or Fairs, Liberties free Customs
Tolls Stallage Pickage, Piepowder Courts —
Fines Amerciaments and all and singular
other the premisses above by these presents
granted or mentioned to be granted, to the
aforesaid George Duke of Buckingham his
heirs & Assignes for ever, and this without
any Account or any other thing from thence
to be given made or paid to Us, Our heirs
or Successors. Wherefore our pleasure is,
and by these presents for Us, or heirs & Successors
We strictly enjoin order & command that the
afores.d George Duke of Buckingham his heirs
& Assigns, by Authority of these presents —
may well freely & lawfully have hold keep —
for ever at the afores.d Town of Wragby the
afores.d Market and the afores.d three separate

11

Feasts or Fairs in and upon the separate days aforesaid respectively together with all & all manner of Liberties Customs Tolls & Profits ____ arising therefrom or with the same or any of them enjoyed according to the Tenor & true Intent of these our Letters Patent without ____ Molestation disturbance grievance or Contradiction of our heirs or Successors or any of them or any of our Sheriffs Escheators Bailiffs Officers or Servants, or of our Successors whatsoever And this without any Warrant Writ or ____ process hereafter to be obtained or procured ____ from Us our Heirs or Successors _____ and altho' no Writ of ___ ad quod Damnum hath issued in this behalf, by reason that Express mention &c In Testimony &c. ____ Witness the King at Westminster the 22. day of Feb.ry in the twenty first Year of The Reign of King Charles the Second _____ By writ of Privy Seal. ____

It agrees with the Record, & is ____
examined by Edm: Warcupp

Unfortunately the Charter was never ratified, allegedly because of an upset between King Charles II and Sir Edmund Turner when the King visited Wragby. It also could have been because shortly after obtaining the Charter, the Duke of Buckingham sold the entire Manor of Wragby to Sir Edmund Turnor for around £5000, to cover his debts to others. Because of the non-ratification, the argument of whether Wragby is a town or a village goes on to this day, although with the earlier arrangement with King Henry III it could be said that we were already a town.

During this period Wragby was extremely prosperous boasting a Glover and a Peruke maker (wigs to you and me) living and working in the area. The population continued to rise until the mid 1800's when a decline began, presumably caused by new agricultural laws from Government and changes in society itself.

One major disadvantage that Wragby had was the fact that it was totally owned by one person - the Lord of the Manor. It was for this reason that Wragby missed the industrial revolution when it was occurring elsewhere. It lagged behind other areas as change was not deemed to be necessary, all was well with the little world of Wragby. Unfortunately, this idyll was blown apart in 1917 when the Turnor family put the estate up for sale.

The result was that Wragby was brought forcibly into the 20th century. Gone was the protection of the Lord of the Manor - people realised that they had to sink or swim. Such was the resilience of the inhabitants most swam. Innovations and enterprises sprang up everywhere and the 'modern' way of doing things was adopted. Businesses adapted well and prospered. Of course, all this took time especially as the sale took place a year before the Great War ended.

Today Wragby is still growing, mainly with housing, as so many people wish to come and live here, and sadly some businesses have closed down. To those new residents Wragby may seem to be a bit behind the times with the pace a little slower than elsewhere. This is understandable as Wragby is still playing catch-up. It is a lovely place to live, a haven in the much stressed world of today and if sometimes it seems you need a stick of dynamite to get things done - now you know why.

An Aerial View of Wragby taken by Mr. W. Marriott

Alterations by Jennifer Dunn - 25th March 1964
Workmen have started to modernise the Turnor Square houses. F. Robinson of Spilsby
are doing the work. Twelve houses are being made into eight.

Changes in the Market Place

Market Place showing Spofforth's Store c.1899

Market Place from Bardney Road c.1908

Market Place c.1937

LORD OF THE MANOR

The Turnor Family

It is a well-known fact that the Turnor family played an enormous part in Wragby for over 200 years. As there has been much written about them elsewhere we present here a condensed version as it pertains to us.

The Turnor dynasty begins in 1674 when the eldest son of the Villiers family, George - 20th Lord Roos, sold Wragby Manor to Sir Edmund Turnor (1619-1707) Baron of the Exchequer. In 1653 Sir Edmund married Margaret, daughter and heir of Sir John Harrison of Stoke Rochford, thereby moving from the South to Lincolnshire. The purchase of Wragby Manor increased Sir Edmund's estates in this area as he consistently purchased other estates in Lincolnshire.

In 1697 Sir Edmund built a chapel and a hospital (almshouses) for 12 persons (six of whom were to be the widows of clergymen, the other six being poor men or women of Wragby). The Bishop of Lincoln, Dr. Gardiner, consecrated the chapel in 1697 and in 1704 Sir Edmund bequeathed to them a yearly rent charge of £100 out of the Manor of Wragby and other estates. He directed that this endowment was to be dispensed yearly as follows: £40 to the Vicar of Wragby for performing services in the chapel; £5 to each widow of poor clergymen occupying six of the hospital houses; £3 6s 8d to each of the six poor widows occupying the other six houses and £10 to be set apart for the reparation of the buildings.

Three years before his death in 1707, Sir Edmund purchased the Manor of Sandon in Wragby, the impropriate rectory of Wragby, the avowson of the vicarage and the free dispensation of the grammar school for the sum of £6000 from Geoffrey Palmer of Carlton Curlieu of Leicestershire. Thus Wragby was united.

By the time of his death, therefore, Sir Edmund was a landlord of considerable standing in the Wragby area having already purchased many of the neighbouring districts.

Sir Edmund's son John inherited the estate, but not for very long due to his father's longevity. John married Diana the only child of Algernon Cecil, son of William, Earl of Salisbury. They had three children; Edmund, Diana and Dorothy. John died in 1719 leaving his son, Edmund II, to reign over the estates for the next 50 years until 1769. He married Elizabeth Ferne, daughter and co heir of Henry Ferne, thereby bringing estates in Derbyshire and Staffordshire into the Turnor family.

Edmund II and Elizabeth also had a son called Edmund who went on to run the estates from 1769 to 1805, when he died at the age of 85. Edmund III married Mary, daughter of John Disney of Lincolnshire, and had four sons and two daughters. Three of the sons and both daughters died between 1760 and 1775. The surviving son was Edmund IV.

Edmund IV is chiefly remembered for his antiquarian pursuits. He became a Fellow of the Society of Antiquaries in 1778 and a Fellow of the Royal Society in 1786. He was also an MP for Midhurst, Sussex from 1802 to 1806. He was married twice. His first wife was Elizabeth, eldest daughter of Philip Broke of Nacton, and they had one daughter. His second wife was Dorothea Tucker and they had a further five sons and two daughters. Like his predecessors, Edmund IV added to the estates with small purchases in Wragby and the surrounding areas.

When Edmund IV died in 1829, at the age of 75, he was succeeded by his son Christopher who was then 20 years old. It was during this time that the Turnor family reached its height of importance and wealth. In a list of Lincolnshire estates in 1870 Christopher was listed fourth with 20,664 acres.

Christopher married into the peerage, his wife being Lady Caroline Finch Hatton, eldest daughter of the 10th Earl of Winchelsea who was the owner of Haverholme Priory near Sleaford. Christopher served as the High Sheriff of Lincolnshire in 1833 and was MP for South Lincolnshire from 1841 to 1847. As well as having a magnificent house built at Stoke Rochford in 1841, designed by architect William Burn, Christopher was responsible for the building of many houses in Wragby itself.

Panton Hall c.1913
The Turnor Family Home

In 1886 Christopher's son, Edmund, succeeded him in more ways than one. Edmund V also married into the peerage. His wife was Lady Mary Gordon, daughter of Charles 10th Marquis of Huntley. Like his father, Edmund V was High Sheriff of Lincolnshire in 1894 and was also an MP for Grantham in 1868 and South Lincolnshire from 1868 to 1880. He retired from politics in 1880 to 'devote himself to the management of his estate in the difficult years which he anticipated lay ahead'.

Edmund V was ever ready to take part in local and county affairs and described himself as a practical agriculturist. He supported the Lincolnshire Agricultural Society and the Lincolnshire Chamber of Agriculture as well as the Lincolnshire Red Shorthorn Association and at various times was chairman of all three bodies. He was also involved with Church affairs.

His wife, also, was heavily involved with philanthropic movements in Lincolnshire and had a strong influence. She founded several habitations of the Primrose League and was Dame President of the Wragby Habitation. She was also President of the Girls Friendly Society and President of the North Lincolnshire Red Cross during the Great War. Lady Mary was awarded a CBE for her public works. She died in 1930.

Edmund V was shooting on the Sibthorp estate, Hatton when he collapsed and died of a heart attack on 15th December 1903. Rather than an elaborate memorial at Stoke Rochford, the restoration of Panton Church was thought more fitting. Lady Mary, Mr. Christopher Turnor (nephew) and other friends and relatives took up this work.

As Edmund V died childless, his brother Christopher Hatton Turnor should have inherited the estates. However he waived this right in favour of his son Christopher Turnor, then aged 30. At that time no one had any idea that within ten years the reign of the Turnor family in Wragby would come to an end.

Although Christopher II was born in Canada he had been educated in England - graduating from Christ Church, Oxford, studied agriculture at Cirencester and practised as an architect. In 1907 he married Sarah Marie Talbot, only daughter and heiress of the Hon. Walter Cecil Carpenter, second son of the 18th Earl of Shrewsbury. With the encouragement of his wife he was involved with many public works covering most aspects of rural life. He not only served on various committees but also wrote numerous articles, for *The Times* and *Country Life,* as well as several books.

Due to economic climes the dissolution of the Turnor estates in North Lincolnshire came in 1917 when the family moved back to Stoke Rochford. Many other estates were also being dispersed at that time, so the sale of Wragby should not be taken in isolation. However its importance locally cannot be overstated.

Wragby Market Place 1916

The sale took place over two days (15th - 16th August) and was conducted in the schoolroom, which had been built by the Turnor's. Christopher II not only gave sitting tenants first refusal but also offered them loans of two-thirds the amount at 5% interest for purchases of land over £1000. He also made over to the residents the water supply and all appertaining to it. There were 163 lots covering 6000 acres and included 22 farms in addition to the smaller Wragby properties. The sale eventually realised over £136,000 (more like millions in today's terms).

We have included a brief résumé of the sale as it appeared in the newspaper of that time on the following pages.

❖ ❖

Wedding Present by Fiona Clark - 11th June 1967
The people of Hansard Drive and Queen Elizabeth Street have collected enough money to give Miss Mary Pickering a lovely clock for a wedding present. She delivers milk on the estate every morning for Mr. Gibson.

The Turnor Family Tree

Sir Edmund Turner (1619-1707) — m — Margaret daughter of Sir John Harrison of Balls, Hertfordshire. Purchased 1653 Stoke Rochford Estate Lincolnshire

John Turnor d. 1719 — m — Diana only child of Algernon Cecil son of William Earl of Salisbury

Diana

Dorothy — m — Rev. George Cousin

Edmund II d. 1769 — m — Elizabeth daughter of Henry Fern of Snitterton Derbyshire

Edmund III d. 1805 — m — Mary daughter of John Disney of Disney Lincolnshire

Others - 3 sons 2 daughters + d. btwn 1760 and 1775

Edmund IV - MP 1754-1829 — m — Elizabeth eldest daughter of Philip Broke of Nacton

— m2 — Dorothea Tucker

daughter

5 boys
2 girls

Frances John

Christopher- MP 1809-1886 — m — Lady Caroline eldest daughter of the 10th Earl of Winchelsea

Christopher Rev. d. 1914

Edmund V JP 1838-1903 — m — Lady Mary daughter of Charles 10th Marquis of Huntley d. 1930

No Issue. Brother Christopher

Waived claim in favour of Son

Christopher Hatton Turner d. 1940 — m 1907 — Sarah Marie Talbot daughter of Hon. Cecil Carpenter 2nd son of 18th Earl of Salisbury

18

Turnor Estate Sale
August 15th and 16th 1917
At the Old School Room Wragby

Lot No.	Description	Purchaser	From	Tenant	£ Paid
1	Brick & Slate Dwelling	Mr. F. Creasey	Wragby	Mr. F. Purchase & Capt. McGowan	550
2	Beech House	Mr. Doughty	Faldingworth	R.W.. Clarke (Dcsd) & Mr. J.H. Robinson	875
3	Brick & Tiled Dwelling + Offices	Mr. Holmes	Wragby	Holmes & Son	450
4	Brick Tiled Dwelling + B'smith shop	Mr. Green	Wragby	Tenant	350
5	Close Grassland	Mr. Holmes	Wragby	Mr. A.E. Bratley	400
6	"B'smith premises, Saddler's Shop" and two Dwelling Houses	Mr. J.B. Johnson	Wragby	Tenant	575
7	Timber Yard and Paddock	Mr. Holmes	Wragby	Holmes & Son + G. Mawer	350
8	Brick & Tiled Residence	Mr. Sales	Lissington	Mrs. Duckering & H. Mawer	400
9	Close Grassland	Mr. J.H. Robinson	Wragby	Tenant	200
10	Close Grassland	Mr. Doughty	Faldingworth	Mr. J.H. Robinson	330
11	Close Grassland	Mr. Doughty	Faldingworth	Mr. F.J. Herbert	160
12	3 Closes Grassland	Mr. Doughty	Faldingworth	J. Robinson & B. Bratley	450
13	Brick & Tiled Cottage	Mr. E.H. Johnson	Wragby	Tenant	150
14	Pleasant Residence	Mr. J.H. Robinson	Wragby	Tenant	280
15	Residence & Business Premises	Mr. J. Bradshaw	Wragby	"Messrs. Whitley, Saggers,"	500
16	Five Cottages	Mr. F. Whitley	Wragby	"Chambers, Priestley and Robinson"	160
17	"Brick & Tiled Residence, Shop" and Bakehouse	Mr. G. Mawer	Wragby	Mr. G. Oswin	375
18	The Manor House	Mr. G. Mawer	Wragby	Messrs. Bratley & Hunter	475
19	Close Grassland	Mr. H. Mawer	Wragby	Mr. J.H. Robinson	150
20	Close Grassland	Mr. J.H. Robinson	Wragby	Berry & Son	170
21	Close Grassland & Arable land	Mr. G. Mawer	Wragby	Messrs. Cottingham & H. Mawer	150
22	Valuable Grassland	Mr. Gast	Wragby	Henry Mawer	280
23	Valuable Grassland	Mr. Whitley	Wragby	I. Robinson	280
24	Allotment Gardens	Mr. Frearson	W. Barkwith	none given	200
25	Three Closes Accommodation land	Mr. F. Creasey	Wragby	Tenant & J.H. Robinson	400
26	Two Closes Accommodation land	Mr. Frearsom	W.Barkwith	Mr. W.J. Berry	190
27	Two Closes Accommodation land	Mr. Frearsom	W.Barkwith	Mr. W.H. Dove	100
28	Three Closes land	Mr. G. Mawer	Wragby	"Messrs. Creasey, Oswin and I. Robinson"	460

Turnor Estate Sale - Page 2

Lot No.	Description	Purchaser	From	Tenant	£ Paid
29	Close Accommodation land	Mr. J. Bradshaw	Wragby	Tenant	130
30	Close Accommodation land	Mr. J. Bradshaw	Wragby	Tenant	290
31	Six Closes Accommodation land	Mr. G. Mawer	Wragby	"Messrs. Barr, Berry, Whitley and C.& E. Greenwood"	550
32	Two Closes Grass land & Two "Cottages, Slaughter House & Farm" Buildings & Stack Yard	Mr. F. Creasey	Wragby	Mr. H.W. Weightman	700
33	Close Accommodation land	Mr. Phillipson	Wragby	Mr. H.W. Weightman	270
34	"Wragby Post Office, Sale Shop and Residence "	Mr. Sutton	Wragby	Tenant	250
35	"The Turnor Arms Hotel, Farm And Farm Buildings"	Mr. Pluck	"Danbury, Chelmsford"	Mr. J. Phillipson	3500
36	Brick & Tiles Business Premises and Dwelling House	Mr. Armstrong	Dewsbury	Messrs. Sutton & Marsden	330
37	Excellent Residence (Fire Station)	Mr. H. Mawer	Wragby	Tenant	400
38	Motor Garage & Cottage	Mr. W.H. Dove	Wragby	Tenant	150
38a	Two Brick & Tiles Dwellings	Holmes & Son	Wragby	Mrs. Trafford & Mrs. Sutton	390
38b	Brick & Tiled Farm Buildings	Mr. H. Mawer	Wragby	Mr. H.W. Weightman	300
39	Row of Five Shops including Reading Room and Cottage at back	Mr. Armstrong	Dewsbury	"Messrs. Berry, Weightman & Son, Brown," "G. Sutton, W. Sutton & H. Mawer"	400
40	Commodious Residence	Mr. G. Mawer	Wragby	Tenant	350
41	"Shop, Dwelling and Business Premises"	Mr. Dove	Wragby	Tenant	150
41a	Brick & Tiled Dwelling	Holmes & Son	Wragby	Mr. I. Robinson	180
42	Close Grassland (Vicarage Field)	Mr. Doughty	Faldingworth	Tennis Club & Rev.W. Moore	300
43	Brick & Plaster Cottage	Mr. Doughty	Faldingworth	Mrs. Nixon	75
44	Two Brick & Tiled Cottages	Mr. Doughty	Faldingworth	Messrs. Barr & Cottingham	290
45	Modern Villa Residence	Mr. F.J. Herbert	Wragby	Tenant	300
45b	Close Grassland	Mr. Robinson	Wragby	Mr. H. Mawer	170
46	Close Accommodation land	Mr. H. Mawer	Wragby	Mr. A. Bratley	210
47	Piece of Garden Ground	Mr. H. Dove	Wragby	Tenant	24

20

Turnor Estate Sale - Page 3

Lot No.	Description	Purchaser	From	Tenant	£ Paid
48	Two Brick & Slated Cottages	Mr. Bratley	Wragby	Tenant & Mrs. Hawks	315
49	Two Accommodation Paddocks	Mr. Bratley	Wragby	Messrs. Marsden & Berry	310
50	Well Situated Dwelling + Land Opp	Mr. J.H. Holmes	Wragby	Tenant	410
51	Brick & Slated Dwelling	Mr. G.H. Cottingham	Wragby	Tenant	310
52	Productive Farm + Bldgs. Opp.	Mr. Ganson	Gainsborough	Mr. J.B. Brothwell	2700
52a	Brick & Tiled Dwelling	Mr. W.J. Berry	Wragby	Tenant	146
52b	Large Accommodation Yard	Holmes & Son	Wragby	Mr. I. Robinson	170
53	Close Grassland	Mrs. Strawson	Metheringham	Mr. J.B. Brothwell	350
54	Accommodation Grass Paddock	Holmes & Son	Wragby	Messrs. C & E Greenwood	90
55	Two Closes Grassland	Holmes & Son	Wragby	Mr. I. Robinson	650
56	Close Accommodation land	Mr. Sales	Lissington	Mr. Wm. Brothwell	200
57	Close of Arable Land	Holmes & Son	Wragby	Allotments	250
58	Close of Arable Land	Mr. Albones	Bardney	Allotments	200
59	Close of Arable Land	Mr. H. Mawer	Wragby	Allotments	75
60	Two Closes Accommodation land	Mr. G. Mawer	Wragby	Tenant	330
61	Four Closes Grass land	Mr. G. Mawer	Wragby	"Messrs. Brothwell, Whitley and Weightman"	550
62	Close Grass Land	Holmes & Son	Wragby	Tenant	240
63	Close Grass Land	Mr. Phillipson	Wragby	C & E Greenwood	160
64	Close of Arable Land	Mr. G. Mawer	Wragby	C & E Greenwood	55
65	Small Holding incl.2 Cottages	Mr. H. Mawer	Wragby	Tenant	1750
66	Close of Grass land	Mr. H. Mawer	Wragby	Mr. J.B.Johnson	90
67	Close of Grass land	Mr. G. Mawer	Wragby	Holmes & Son	65
68	Close of Arable Land	Mr. G. Mawer	Wragby	Mr. B. Bratley	150
69	Three Enclosures Grass Land	Mr. G. Mawer	Wragby	Mr. G.D. Barr	390
70	Holme Hill + Hallbush Wood	Mr. Burton	Bardney	Mr. C.F. Puttergill	1150
71	Primrose Hill + Badgermoor Wood	Mr. Albones	Bardney	"Messrs. Bratley, G.Robinson, and H. Mawer"	2200
72	Two Closes Grass land	Mr. W.H. Bradshaw	Wragby	E.H. & W. Johnson	235
73	Two Closes Grass land	Holmes & Son	Wragby	Tenant	280
74	Two Closes Grass land	Mr. W.F. Mawer	Goltho	Mr. J.B. Johnson	220
75	Close of Grass land	Mr. W. Brothwell	Wragby	Tenant	115
76	Three Closes Grass land	Mr. G. Mawer	Wragby	B.Bratley & G. Robinson	825
77	Close of Grass land	Mr. J.B. Johnson	Wragby	Tenant	200
78	Brick & Tiled Cottage	Mr. W. Brothwell	Wragby	Tenant	120

Turnor Estate Sale - Page 4

Lot No.	Description	Purchaser	From	Tenant	£ Paid
79	Compact Farm (228a) known as Barn Farm	Mr. Pluck	Danbury, Chelmsford	Miss F. Harrison, Mr. A. Harrison and Mr. H. Weightman	3750
		End of First Day's Sale		**Total**	**£38,170**
80	Convenient Farm (Barkwith Road)	Mr. Bucknall	Grimsby	Mr. H.W. Weightman	1825
81	Two Closes Grass + Close Arable	Mr. W. Jarrett	Wragby	Tenant	800
82	Two Closes Grass land	Mr. W. Jarrett	Wragby	Tenant	300
83	Close of Grass land	Mr. Motson	Holton Beckering	Mr. G. Sutton	325
84	Piece Accommodation land	Mr. G. Sutton	Wragby	Tenant	100
85	Building Site + Orchard	Mr. G. Sutton	Wragby	Tenant	30
86	Desirable Small Holding	Mr. Phillipson	Wragby	Mr. E. Marsden	1530
87	Stretch Useful land	Withdrawn at £616		Messrs. Whitley, Barr, Brothwell & Weightman	
88	Five Closes Grass land	Withdrawn at $500 later sold			
		To Mr. G. Mawer		Messrs. Sutton, Berry, & I. Robinson	600
89	Close of Grass land	Mr. J. Bradshaw	Wragby	Tenant	120
90	Close of Feeding land	Mr. Hill	Caldwell	Mr. H.W. Weightman	1500
91	Dwelling and Farm Premises	Mr. Phillipson	Wragby	Mr. H.W. Weightman	375
92	Yard, Premises & Garden - also 93			Mr. W. J. Berry	
93	Farm Premises & Stackyard	Mr. Frearson	W. Barkwith	Mr. E. Marsden	475
94	Two Brick & Slated Cottages	Mr. Dickinson	Tattershall	Messrs. J. Wherry & C. Whitley	300
95	Builders Yard with Lot 45	Mr. I. F. Herbert		Tenant	
96	Brick & Slate Cottage	Mr. G. Mawer	Wragby	Mr. J.W. Thorn	270
97	Brick & Slate Cottage (Occ.2)	Miss Phillipson	Wragby	Mr. W. Buffham & Miss Phillipson	300
98	Four Brick & Slated Cottages	Mr. Albones	Bardney	Messrs. Whitely, Weightman, Parrish, Sharp, J. Phillipson and Miss Harrison	825
99	Block Four Modern Cottages	Mr. Phillipson	Wragby	Messrs. Weightman, Paddison, Brothwell and Broxholme	550
100	Block Four Modern Cottages	Mr. Dickinson	Tattershall	Messrs. Hill, Bradley, Johnson & Barr	525
101	Brick Built Tower Mill	Mr. H. Mawer	Wragby	Tenant	50
102	Piece Garden Ground	Mr. Phillipson	Wragby	Mr. G. Mawer	21
103	Four Brick & Slated Bungalows	Mr. Dickinson	Tattershall	Messrs. Broxholme, Kirk, Cunnington & Colton	325

Turnor Estate Sale – Page 5

Lot No.	Description	Purchaser	From	Tenant	£ Paid
104	Two Brick & Slated Cottages	Mr. Dickinson	Tattershall	Messrs. E. Thorn and J. Holmes & Son	250
105	Three Brick & Tiled Cottages	Mr. Dickinson	Tattershall	"Messrs. Wheatley, Brothwell & Taylor"	50
106	Two Brick & Tiled Cottages	Mr. A.T. Bratley	Wragby	Messrs.H.W. Weightman & H. Ealand	310
107	Pair Modern Cottages	Mr. I. Robinson	Wragby	Messrs. Kitchen and Hawks	310
108	Pair Modern Cottages	Mr. Buffham	Wragby	Messrs. Baker and Scaife	325
150	Wire Hill Farm (Panton Parish)	Mr. N. Cook	Wragby	Tenant	4900

End of Wragby Sale incl. Wire Hill Farm

Total Second Day £17,291

Total Sale Price for Wragby £55,461

The Whole Estate Realised £136,046

During the auction of the Panton Estate, Lot 150 Wire Hill Farm, comprising farmhouse, farm buildings, two cottages and 285 acres of land came up for sale, and a newspaper reported

" A dispute respecting a bid cost a farmer £650 at the second day's auction sale of the Panton estate at Wragby last week. A farm of 285 acres was knocked down to the tenant for £4250, when a gentleman in the company called out that was his bid. " I took the gentleman's bid over there, " said the auctioneer. The gentleman repeated that he had bid £4250, and the auctioneer then said that as there was a dispute he would put the property up again. Thereupon a spirited " duel " took place between the two would-be purchases, the tenant eventually acquiring the lot at £4900. The episode only lasted about a minute ".

The tenant who purchased the farm was Nimrod Cooke grandfather of John Winn, one of the now older residents in Wragby, schooled in Wragby, and who spent most, if not all of his working life on the farm.

The farm, as it was, now comprises Panton Grange (the old farmhouse now a private residence), the converted farm buildings (another private residence) and about 4 acres of land including a small spinney.

Turnor Estate Sale - Appendix

Principal Purchasers
(Most from Wragby unless otherwise stated)

Name	£ Paid	Area if not Wragby
Mr. Pluck	7250	Danbury, Chelmsford
Mr. N. Cook	4900	
Mr. H. Mawer	3025	
Mr. Ganson	2700	Gainsborough
Holmes & Son	2250	
F. Creasey	1650	
Mr. Hill	1500	Caldwell
Mr. Burton	1150	Bardney
Mr. J. Bradshaw	1040	
Mr. Bratley	935	
Mr. J.B. Johnson	775	
Mr. Sales	600	Lissington
Mr. Sutton	380	
Mr. Green	350	
Mr. Buffham	325	
Mr. G.H. Cottingham	310	
Mr. F.J. Herbert	300	
Mr. Gast	280	
Mr. W. Brothwell	235	
Mr. E.H. Johnson	150	

Name	£ Paid	Area if not Wragby
Mr. G. Mawer	5595	
Mr. Albones	3225	Bardney
Mr. Phillipson	2906	
Mr. Doughty	2480	Faldingworth
Mr. Bucknall	1825	Grimsby
Mr. J.H. Holmes	1610	
Mr. Dickinson	1450	Tattershall
Mr. Jarrett	1100	
Mr. Frearson	965	West Barkwith
Mr. J.H. Robinson	820	
Mr. Armstrong	730	Dewsbury
Mr. F. Whitley	440	
Mrs. Strawson	350	Metheringham
Mr. Motson	325	Holton Beckering
Mr. W.H. Dove	324	
Mr. I. Robinson	310	
Miss Phillipson	300	
Mr. W.H. Bradshaw	235	
Mr. W.F. Mawer	220	Goltho
Mr. W.J. Berry	146	

Total   **£55,461**

EDUCATION AND LEARNING

The Ladies Seminary

The forerunner of the Ladies Seminary was probably the boarding and day academy run by Eliza Blundy listed in 1835. There were, however, many privately run schools in the area at that time, mostly comprising a governess/teacher and one or two pupils.

Sisters Caroline and Martha Blundy opened the Ladies Seminary in the Market Place in 1837. They were the daughters of Richard Blundy, who had been headmaster of the Free Grammar School, and so were well versed in educational needs. As near as we can tell, the Seminary was located above what is now the Pet Shop and the St. Barnabas shop.

Between 1841 and 1851 Martha married and moved to Binbrook leaving Caroline to run the school with the assistance of younger sister Sarah. Eventually Sarah left and Caroline ran it on her own.

The Seminary not only had local day pupils but also boarders from all parts of the county. The curriculum included grammar and geography and, more importantly, the social graces; drawing, music (piano), needlework and ballroom dancing. Lessons were held mainly in one room during the hours of 9 o'clock - noon and 2 - 4 o'clock. There were no examinations or inspections although Lady Mary Turnor visited occasionally and the Vicar attended every Monday to take scripture lessons.

In about 1871, after the death of her husband, Martha returned to the Seminary along with her daughter also called Martha. Shortly afterwards Caroline's sister, Martha, died.

At the close of the century the school was still under the charge of Caroline Blundy. As she was slipping into her dotage it was effectively run by her nieces, Martha and Mary Anne Croft.

There were only about eight girls, of whom two or three were boarders. In 1902, the pupils took one of the few school trips to the Palestine Exhibition in Lincoln. They attended Church during Lent and on feast days and traditionally decorated the church for Easter.

Caroline Blundy was highly respected but eccentric. She bore a superficial resemblance to Queen Victoria and was known to sit for hours wearing the sombre colours and a small white lace cap associated with the Queen. (She was not the only imitator of Royalty – Stationmaster Thomas Saggers cultivated a resemblance to Edward VII). A pupil played cards with her in the evening with strict instructions to let her win. She died in 1904, aged 91, bequeathing the Seminary to her nieces.

Martha Croft was tall and rather severe while Mary Anne was stout and friendly. It is alleged that Mary Anne was a secret drinker and that both were being courted by a schoolmaster from East Barkwith, albeit in a desultory fashion.

The Ladies Seminary survived with falling numbers until around 1913. It had lasted for approximately 80 years and was a place where a few generations of country girls aspired to the graces and accomplishments normally attained by the gentry.

Free Grammar School

In 1627 William Hansard of Biscathorpe made a provision in his will for the setting up of free Grammar schools in both Caistor and Wragby. In 1632, Wragby Free Grammar School was founded. It was endowed with a yearly rent charge of £30 out of an estate at Bilsby, for the instruction of the youth of the parish (about 20 boys) in literature and the rudiments of religion.

The building was allowed to deteriorate but rebuilt by Edmund Turner in 1775, at the expense of the parish. The fact that the building had been allowed to sink into a state of decay says much about the importance of education at that time. However, in the directory of 1792 it states that 'here is an excellent free school'. It also lists Enos Moody as Master.

One notable pupil was Thomas Espin who went on to become headmaster of Mapletoft Free State School, known as The English Charity School, in Louth. He renamed his school The Mathematical, Nautical, Architectural and Commercial Academy. Thomas Espin was an acclaimed mathematician, architect and artist; he also completed text books on English and Mathematics which were subsequently published. An artist of considerable ability he won the Fellowship of the Society of Antiquarians in 1813. As a person of standing, he drew up plans for the new Town Hall in Louth. Unfortunately this was never built and as compensation Espin received the stone with which he built 'Gothic Cottage'. Within the grounds he built his own Mausoleum and was interred there in 1822. Gothic Cottage is now The Priory, a well known hotel.

Pupils Gardening at the Old Grammar School 1908

Richard Blundy was appointed headmaster in 1804. To supplement his meagre stipend he took in boarders and sold stationery and other goods. On his death in 1837 Christopher Turnor appointed Blundy's son, Thomas, as headmaster and also made provision for Blundy's daughters, Martha and Caroline, to open the Ladies Academy.

Mismanagement of the school and a lack of facilities to teach the poor of the parish caused John Turnor and his sister Frances to build a National School, at their own expense, on land given to them by Christopher Turnor in 1839. A headmaster's residence was built the following year by Christopher Turnor. The school was initially used as a Grammar and Parochial school for boys and in 1871 was united with the Free Grammar school which was then being used as a girls Parochial school.

By 1885 the Free Grammar school was used as a Sunday School, and in the early 1900's it was used by Mr. Banks to hold technical classes in the winter and gardening in the spring/summer.

The school eventually held the reception class of the National School and many residents remember starting their schooling there. Miss Pickering also held classes there for older children who had originally started at the National School. It was finally closed as a school in 1969 although some clubs and organisations used the building for quite awhile afterwards.

The building, located next to the surgery and resource centre, became so dilapidated and uninhabitable that it was sold. Today it has been sympathetically restored as a private residence and the original plinth can be seen above the front porch.

The National School

As stated previously this school was built at the expense of John and Francis Turnor on land given to them by Christopher Turnor, Lord of the Manor. He supplemented the original endowment of £30, from William Hansard, by another £30 annual subscription. Funds also came from a voluntary rate by the parishioners, Government grants and the School pence.

In 1871, it became known as 'Wragby Church of England School' with 130 children attending by 1872.

It is difficult to say with any certainty who was the first headmaster as both Thomas Blundy and John Bowlden are listed as schoolmasters on the 1841 census. However, by 1851 John Turney was headmaster and was residing at the school master's house. He was also taking in boarders presumably to augment his stipend.

National School and Headmaster's Residence

It would appear from the records that the annual grants were given on the numbers of children attending the school. As the table below shows there was a definite decline between 1873 and 1883.

	1873	1883
Mr. Turnor	£30	£25
Parishioners Rate	£19 2s 10d	£17 11s 4d
Government	£69 8s 0d	£44 12s 0d
School Pence	£79 19s 8d	£32 14s 8d

At this time – 1873 – William Dodds was the headmaster and the school thrived under his guardianship. Payment had improved somewhat from the early days, and Mr. Dodds was paid an annual salary of £75. He also received a share of the Government grant amounting to £21 10s 3d and a portion of the School Pence amounting to £65 2s 6d; a total sum of £161 12s 9d. A qualified teacher was paid £20 and a portion of the School Pence, and an Articled Pupil Teacher was paid £11.

William Musgrave succeeded Mr. Dodds around 1881 and by 1885 the number of children attending the school was down to just 60 pupils. Probably the most innovative headmaster was Herbert J. Banks who had succeeded Mr. Musgrave by 1891. As much is said of Mr. Banks elsewhere, it is sufficient to say that under his leadership the number of children attending the school had risen to 115 by 1896.

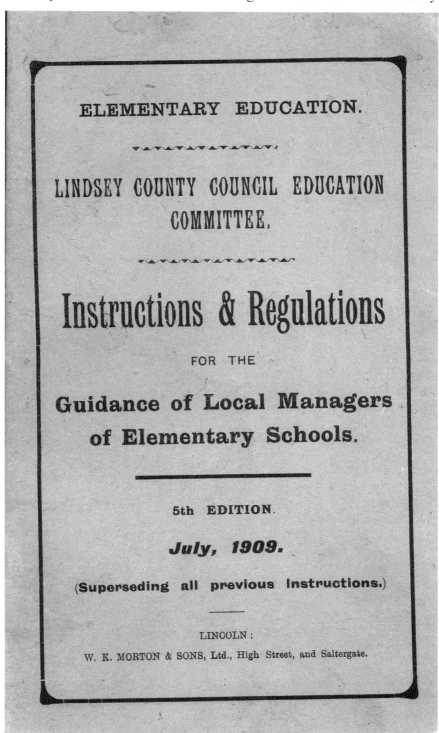

The school was taken over by Lindsey County Council in 1909 and strict rules were laid down and published in a booklet by the Education Committee to avoid confusion.

Special Byelaws for Rural Districts existed within these rules regarding attendances; it was possible for parents to apply for total or partial exemptions. Total exemption could be granted to children between the ages of 12 and 14, who were beneficially employed and who met certain criteria, to cease attending school. Partial exemption meant children could be exempt from school during the period 1st May to 10th September. This would have allowed children to help with the family business and was therefore looked

31

III.—Precedure under which Exemption Certificates are granted.

SPECIAL EXAMINATIONS FOR LABOUR CERTIFICATES.

H.M. Inspector will hold special examinations for those desirous of obtaining Certificates of having reached or passed the standards required by the Bye-laws at the places, and during the months mentioned, in the following list.

Notice of the actual time, date, and place will be issued to all schools in the district concerned one month before each examination.

No examinations will be held unless there are ten candidates.

Forms for sending in lists of candidates can be obtained from any School Attendance Officer, or from the Secretary. They must be returned to the Secretary at least one week before the date fixed for the examination.

LIST OF SPECIAL EXAMINATIONS.

Place.	Month.	Place.	Month.
Alford	May	Kirton-in-Lindsey	May
Althorpe	October	Lincoln	October
Bardney	June	Louth	July
Barton-on-Humber	November	Mablethorpe	May
Binbrook	February	Market Rasen	October
Brigg	January	Normanby-by-Spital	May
Caistor	April	North Thoresby	October
Cleethorpes	May	Saxilby	May
Coningsby	January	Scunthorpe	June
Crowle	April	South Somercotes	March
Epworth	April	Spilsby	December
Gainsborough	September	Stickney	May
Habrough	April	Tetford	April
Hogsthorpe	November	Wainfleet	June
Horncastle	July	Wragby	December

BYELAW 5 (a).—After each Labour Examination, the Result Schedules are sent in by His Majesty's Inspector to this Office. A copy of the schedule is thereupon sent to the School Correspondent, together with a Certificate (Form S.A. 22) for each child found to have qualified for exemption. A list of the names of those so qualified is at the same time forwarded to the School Attendance Officer.

If not satisfied as to age, the School Attendance Officer must demand a Birth Certificate before regarding a child as free from obligation to attend school.

upon as learning a trade. To be eligible for partial exemption children had to be 11 years of age and total exemption could be granted at 13.

Mr. Mumby

When Mr. Banks was forced to leave, by Mr. Dove and Mr. Robinson (both Non-Conformist members of the Committee), in 1917, the position of headmaster was given to Mr. Mumby. *(Note the anomaly of a Church of England school being effectively governed by two Methodists)* A talented musician, Mr. Mumby used to make his own musical instruments including his cello, and was involved with the Wragby Minstrels. Mr. Mumby was headmaster at the school until 1952 when Mr. Bones succeeded him; a total of 35 years.

Old School c.1960

When Mr. Bones was headmaster, his class was in the middle of the building. There were no corridors and pupils had to walk through one classroom to get to the next. As Mr. Bones didn't have a secretary, the telephone was in the classroom and he would often answer it during lessons. Every week or two he gave the pupils a test and they had to sit in the order that they were marked. The one with the best marks sat in the front right desk and the pupils with the lowest marks were sat in the bottom left area of the classroom.

With the expansion of the village, the National School was no longer adequate and the older children were eventually sent to schools in Horncastle and Market Rasen. A new primary school was built in Silver Street which opened in 1968, with Mr. Richard Bones as headmaster. Since that time it has had only two other headmasters; Mr. Chris Burbage (1978 to 1993) and Mr. Roger Holbrook (1994 to present). Mrs. Naylor was Acting Head in the period July 1993 and January 1994.

The school continued with Mr. Banks' policy of teaching pupils to swim when sufficient funds were raised to build their own swimming pool, which has been written about elsewhere. In 2005 and 2006 pupils at the school displayed their gardening skills by winning prizes in the Wragby in Bloom competitions. Worthy successors indeed to the pupils of 100 years ago who were taught these skills by Mr. Banks.

The new Primary School

Mr. Herbert J. Banks

Herbert James Banks was born in Kent in 1862 and retired in 1922 after 40 years as Headmaster - 28½ years of which was spent at Wragby School. He was a man of many talents, full of boundless enthusiasm, determined and vigorous in his work.

Perhaps the most innovative Headmaster of his time in the whole country, Mr. Banks presided over the National School from 1888 to 1917. During this time he not only overcame severe staffing difficulties but also, in the days of 'payment by results', managed to obtain the highest grants available for the school. He also pioneered the idea of practical education, incorporating carpentry and gardening into his curriculum .

Lessons were held in both the National School and the Old Grammar School; the garden of the latter was used for practical lessons. Shortly after Mr. Banks' arrival in Wragby, the management of the school was overhauled and instead of being dominated by the gentry and clergy a more democratic group, elected by the ratepayers, was put in place. The original managers were Mr. J.B. Johnson (Blacksmith), Mr. T. Cockett (Grocer), Mr. J. Weightman (Butcher), Mr. J.H. Holmes (Wheelwright) and Mr. J.F. Priestley (Plumber). The vicar remained as chairman but without much status. Relations between Mr. Banks and this committee were fairly good as they agreed to many of his requests. These included the separation of the roles of Church Organist and Schoolmaster (he was organist at All Saints Church for many years) and the building of extensions to the National School – with some pressure from the Squire, Edmund Turnor.

The School had a bank (The Penny Bank) which was established in 1891. The vicar persuaded the majority of parents to continue paying what had been the old School Pence into a new savings bank. The local MP, Mr. Perks, and Mr. Turnor both contributed to the bank.

The schoolrooms were used 'out of hours' for a number of different purposes, including dances, and in 1893 Mr. Banks started an evening 'Continuation School' which was intended for adults. However, it was mainly young boys who attended. The subjects taken included carpentry, arithmetic, history, geography, drawing, music, gardening and needlework. In 1895 fees were introduced. Initially these were returned in the form of prizes for attendance but they were later given for performance as well. The school inspectors spoke highly of this endeavour in both teaching and content. Indeed some of Mr. Banks' pupil-teachers attended to further their own education.

Swimming was another of Mr. Banks' interests that he passed on to his pupils. After saving the life of William Mawer in Sudbroke Lake and discovering he was the only swimmer out of a party of 120 people, Mr. Banks was determined to add swimming to the curriculum. With the help of volunteers and scholars he constructed a permanent dam in the beck and also built a dressing shed with two rooms to facilitate mixed bathing. There he taught swimming and life saving. He introduced life saving certificates, which were presented by Lady Mary Turnor who was an avid supporter of the scheme.

Although not everyone approved, the scheme was justified when, in the Great War, the troopship 'Mercian' was torpedoed in 1917 and all the Wragby contingent of the Lincolnshire Yeomanry, who were on board, survived while many others perished. One ex-pupil of Mr. Banks survived for 17 hours in the water.

Other subjects introduced by Mr. Banks included cycling proficiency, woodcarving and cooking. As he was secretary of the Annual Flower Show and a keen gardener, gardening was also introduced and he

Edith Banks with her daughter in 1892

Note the Victorian Pushchair

directed his pupils to build their own greenhouse as part of the woodworking lessons. Their efforts eventually won prizes.

Apart from school life Mr. Banks was well known in other fields. He was renowned throughout the county as an authority on beekeeping and was also in demand for his land measurement skills as well as his musical talents. It was primarily due to Mr. Banks that one of Wragby's thriving industries was born.

Mr. Banks was a crack shot and a member of Wragby Rifle Club. He was also famous for his prize-winning photographs and won hundreds of prizes for flowers, fruit and honey plus cups and medals for sports.

Mrs. Banks and Daughters relaxing in the School Gardens c.1913

It was possible that his popularity provoked envy in one of the managers of the school, rope maker, Joseph Robinson, who was elected for the first time in 1895. Although failing to get re-elected, he returned to the managing committee by another route in 1903 after a further change in the school's status. He subsequently became a thorn in Mr. Banks' side aided by Mr. W.H. Dove. Messrs. Robinson & Dove constantly made life difficult for Mr. Banks – failing to inform him of information received from the County Education Committee or other outside bodies and blocking requests for extra staff. The situation became untenable and in 1917 in a fit of pique Mr. Banks tendered his resignation, which was gleefully accepted by Mr. Robinson.

There was an emotional farewell ceremony on 4th April, at which most of the village paid their respects. Mr. Banks received some magnificent testimonials and gifts, which included a revolving armchair and revolving book cabinet. On 11th April, regretting his impulse, Mr. Banks left the school for good. Mr. Robinson's delight lasted not four days as he then received a letter – in his capacity as Parish Council Chairman - from Christopher Turnor advising the Council that he was selling his Wragby Estates.

Mr. Banks, meanwhile, had taken a post at Boultham Council School, from where he retired in 1922. He continued as a Lay Reader, taking sermons in various parishes, until he had a serious accident in 1933. Mr. Banks subsequently died, aged 72, on 7th September 1934 .

School Boys playing on grassed playground c.1908

Bees by Hilary Thorne - 19th June 1964
On Wednesday Mr. Bones' class came to see our bees. They all put on our new nets. Nobody got stung.

ALL THINGS MEDICAL

Physicians and Surgeons

The best known landmark of a doctor's presence in Wragby is probably Wrangham House, which is situated on the Lincoln to Skegness road opposite the Turnor Arms. Originally the house was connected to the surgery next door via a connecting door which can still be seen as can the old door bell. The properties are both now individual premises, privately owned, and Wrangham House is being sympathetically restored by the current owners.

Wrangham House c.1930

However, there was a surgery held in the Market Place in the region of what is now the Corn Dolly and later further down the Bardney Road adjacent to where the Wragby Plastics entrance was. It is difficult to pinpoint with any accuracy where the earlier Market Place surgeries were, as the old censuses did not give names to buildings but just identified entries as Market Place, including Wrangham House.

The earliest known doctors in the area were Charles Sutton and William Walls who are listed in the Directory of 1792. Where they practised is unclear for the reasons given above. Charles had a son in 1801, also called Charles and to differentiate between the two, the son was called Frederick or Charles Frederick. In 1828 Charles Frederick was listed as a Tea Dealer and Druggist but had become a surgeon in his own right by 1835, by which time Charles senior had retired. At that time William Wrangham came on the scene and it is presumed he practised in Wrangham House.

By 1841 William's brother John had joined him in the practice and Charles Frederick Sutton was still a chemist and druggist as well as a surgeon. Charles Sutton the elder died in 1844 and sometime after 1851 Charles Frederick left Wragby for London. To mark the occasion he was given a luncheon in his honour at the Turnor Arms. He was presented with a silver tea urn by C.F. Heneage, Esq. MP and the Rev. W.K. Marshall presented Mrs. Sutton with a silver waiter, showing how well they were thought of.

William Wrangham died in 1853 and his brother, John, was joined by John Dean Baker. This partnership lasted until 1873 when Dr. Baker died, followed by John Wrangham in 1875.

Frederick Hall took over the practice and was also the Medical Officer for the district. By 1889 Dr. Hall had left for Hampshire and Edward/Edmund Barry Denny had taken over. Such was the power of the Squires in those days that an unwilling Dr. Denny was forced to move to East Barkwith in 1896 to be closer to Lady Mary Turnor.

Geoffrey Colley March was then the resident GP in 1901, having come from Manchester where he was a student of medicine. A story about Dr. March tells of the time when he used to ride a horse to his home visits (as all doctors did). Apparently he was used to tying his horse to a rail when he went into a house but on one occasion the police prosecuted him as it was illegal to leave a horse on a public road unattended. From then on it is said that he took his horse into the kitchen with him whenever he made a visit.

Dr. March was followed by William Deane around 1909. William was the son of Dr. Samuel Deane, whose practice was in Scothern. As both William and his brother George, also a doctor, served during WWI we are uncertain who covered the area in their absence, possibly Dr. Denny and Dr. S. Deane.

After the war George Deane was resident GP at Wrangham House until about 1927 when Dr. Coutts took over until about 1931. He, in turn was followed by a Dr. Hunt. Unfortunately Dr. Hunt's wife could not settle in Wragby and made him move to a more socialised area where she could continue with her social life.

Doctor Roe came to Wrangham House in 1933 on what was supposedly a long lease but turned out to be only two years! He was then told he had to buy the house. In his words *"this was most unwelcome as it was much too big for a young doctor starting out, and my wife did not like it at all. Fortunately for me, just at that time there was a fire at Holmes Wood yard which had involved the house – slightly, but Mrs. Holmes refused to live there again and eventually they went to live in Bardney. Mr. Holmes, somehow hearing of my need for a house, offered me Rehoboth and volunteered all sorts of work to fit me up with a surgery. As it turned out he was disappointed by the Insurance Company, who refused to meet his claim in full. He had not carried out some works which had been demanded when the policy was taken out, in particular a wall should have been built between the house and garden and the timber yard. This was built after the fire. Anyway I had to manage with a coal house and some other offices as surgery and dispensary."*

When shown the picture of Wrangham House, illustrated at the beginning of this chapter, Dr. Roe thought that it could have been taken anytime between the late 1920's or 1930's but did not recognise either of the maids. *"When I came here in 1933 I engaged Ethel Whitehead and the Priestley girl but I don't think either of the girls shown are Ethel or Priestley. This means that the photograph must have been taken earlier than 1931 because I inherited Ethel from Dr. Hunt who preceded me."*

Wrangham house remained empty for some years. A Mr. Scaife, whose son worked as a driver for Holmes Woodyard occupied it for a time and it was eventually sold to Mr. Albert Dove. Mr. and Mrs. Woolgar, the local newsagent, lived there from 1969 to 1997. At some point it was turned into student accommodation and became a rundown shell. It has currently been sold and as stated previously the new owners are in the process of restoring the house that for so many years served the doctors of the community.

Dr. W. Browne came to Wragby in 1950 to join Dr. Roe who had now been at the practice for 17 years. At this time the surgery was in the Corn Dolly area and continued there until 1965 when the Doctors moved to Bardney Road. The surgery proved to be too small and cramped and after a few years new surgeries were built in Silver Street and Torrington Lane, East Barkwith. Both buildings had their own parking spaces outside and inside was a nurses room, reception area and consulting room.

Dr. Roe retired in March 1972 leaving Dr. Brown as senior partner and for a few years he was joined by Dr. Smiley. In 1975 Dr. Richard Starbuck joined what was now a large practice covering an area from Donnington on Bain, and Ludford to the east.

When Dr. Brown retired in 1980, Dr. Starbuck carried on single handedly until he was joined by Dr. Watson. However, Dr. Watson left in 1981 to start his own surgery in the wooden bungalow on Victoria Street. He retired in 1997.

Dr. Starbuck was then joined by a female doctor, Dr. Cox, who stayed for some time. In 1995, Dr. Starbuck was tragically killed in a motoring accident while returning home after visiting a patient. Doctors Owen and Smith then took over the practice with Dr. Whitbread and in the millennium year a new surgery was opened in Old Grammar School Way and the Silver Street one closed. Doctor Owen moved back to Tetford and Dr. Smith left to be replaced by Dr. Rhodes.

The New Surgery and Resource Centre

The new building also holds a resource centre, with computer access for all, and was a joint project made possible by Lincolnshire County Council and Dr. R. Whitbread.

Whilst all the doctors are held in high esteem, Dr. Starbuck, in particular, is still mentioned with great affection. He is remembered with a memorial plaque in the Market Place and a seat in East Barkwith outside the Village Hall.

District Nurses

Since the nursing profession came to the fore with Florence Nightingale nurses have consistently worked hand in hand with doctors. The first recorded nurse in Wragby was Mary Squire in 1841, although at 65 she had probably retired.

In the late 1920's and early 1930's Sister Mary Walton had a nursing and maternity home in Bardney Road. Nurse Thorne and Nurse Ormand also practised in Wragby before 1960.

Since then the role of nurses in the community has changed considerably. There are now Practice nurses, District/Community nurses, Health Care Assistants, Health Visitors and Nurse Practitioners all working with the local doctors from the surgery.

Isolation Hospital

About a mile out of Wragby, on the Bardney Road and across a field, stands the derelict remains of the old Isolation Hospital. Now in a complete state of disrepair, it was built in 1850. It was necessary to build well away from the village as it was intended to treat patients who had contracted tuberculosis, smallpox and other contagious diseases in the Victorian period. It is not known when the hospital was closed but it ended its days serving the community as a maternity hospital.

During WWII a search light battery was stationed there, adjacent to the Bardney- Louth railway line. Close by the hospital is the remains of a mud and stud house, the last occupant of which was a smallholder Mr. Joe Blunt and his family.

The Red Cross

Elsie Draper recalls her time with the Wragby Red Cross.

The Old Grammar School at Wragby was used during the war by the Red Cross and many people from Wragby were members. Nurse Thorne and Nurse Quincy gave us instruction and Dr. Roe used to ask questions. We had all the equipment such as bandages, stretchers, etc. Certificates were given for First Aid and Home Nursing.

Among the members at that time were: Mrs. Mawer, Miss Amy Mawer, Miss Ella Mawer, Mrs. Bygott, Mrs. Rutland, Miss Edna Wright, Miss Daphne Rounce, Miss Marjorie Burnett, Miss Marjorie Smeaton and myself – Elsie Draper.

Members of the British Red Cross Wragby Branch - 1916

AT PRAYER

In Wragby today there are two places of worship, the church of All Saints, which caters to members of the Church of England, and a Methodist Church.

All Saints

The Old Church

Wragby Church
Drawing by Nattes 1790

From the Local Studies Collection, Lincoln Central Library
by courtesy of Lincolnshire County Council

Nothing is left of this Norman church which was situated in the old cemetery. It was built around 1220 AD, replacing an older Saxon church, conveniently next to the Manor house mentioned in the Domesday Book and the surrounding peasant houses. This was the centre of old medieval Wragby.

From the records we can determine that from 1220 until 1233 various squires were the patrons of the church. In 1233 the de Ross (Roos) family took over the patronage of the church until 1349 when Irford Priory took control. The church was officially appropriated to Irford Priory in 1403 and a vicarage was ordained at the same time. The Priory kept control for the next 200 years or so until the Grantham family regained control around 1617. The patronage passed to Sir Edmund Turnor when he purchased the estate in 1674.

The church had a tower measuring 48 feet high, a nave with late Norman columns, an aisle to its north and a south porch of brick. The chancel was originally of stone, having its own north aisle, and was used as a Lady Chapel. However as the chapel was used by 'idle people and boys to loiter in' at service time, it was pulled down and replaced by a brick chancel in 1756 by Edmund Turnor, Esq.

Selection of Drawings depicting different aspects of the old Church
The originals of which are held by All Saints Church

Time moved on and as frequently happened in post medieval Britain, the centre of the town moved. The church fell into decay and was listed in one Directory as being '*an ancient structure situated at an inconvenient distance*'. Given the circumstances the Lord of the Manor and many others petitioned the Bishop to build a new church.

The old church was demolished except for the chancel which was then used as a chapel for burial purposes. The Queen signed a redundancy order on 7th February 1980 and the chancel was demolished in 1981.

The Chancel during demolition

The New Church

As mentioned previously, when it was determined that the old church could no longer serve the requirements of the parish a petition was sent to the Bishop of Lincoln asking permission for a new, more conveniently located, church to be built. The petition and the Bishop's formal reply are illustrated to give an idea of the seriousness and formality that was required.

First page of the Petition

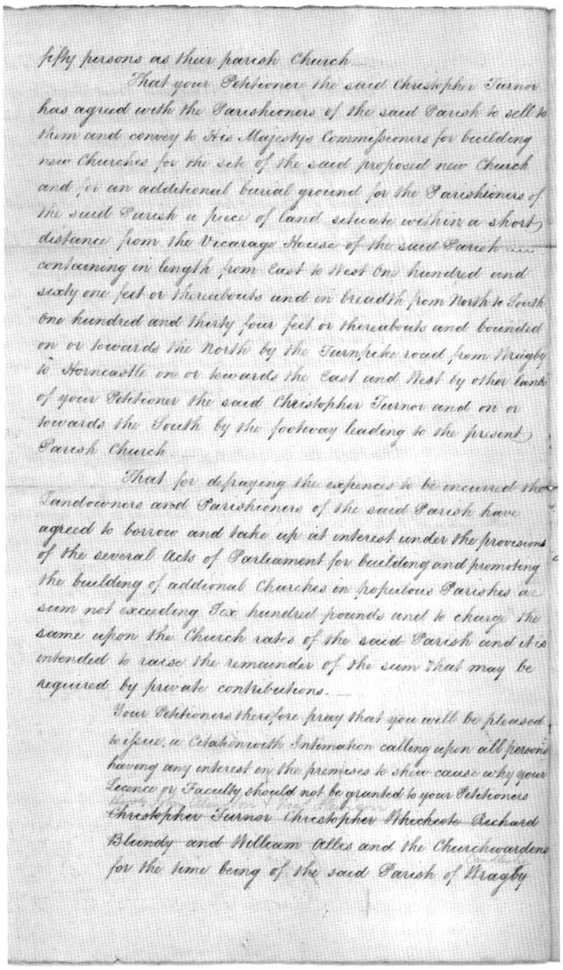

Pages 2 and 3 of the Petition

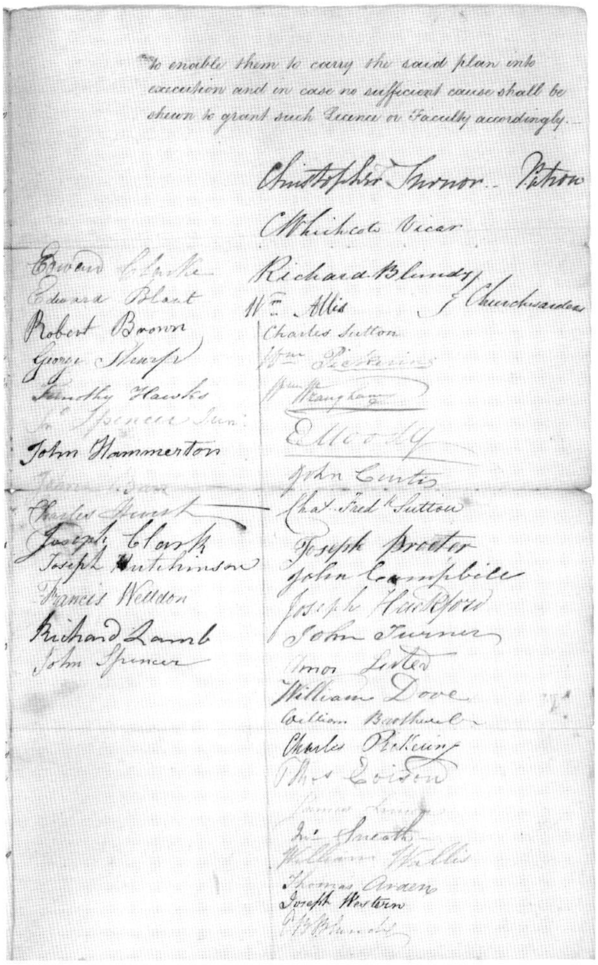

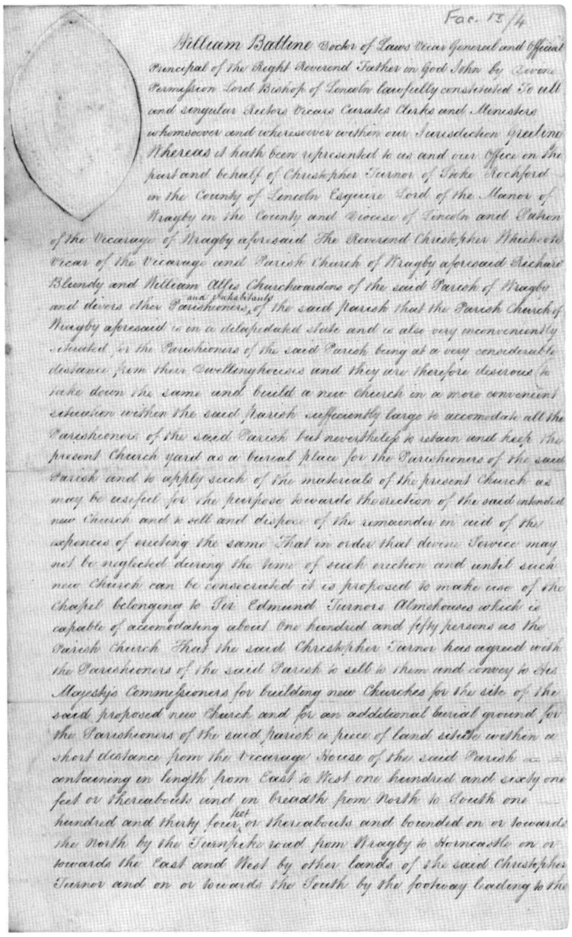

Pages 1 and 2 of the Permission

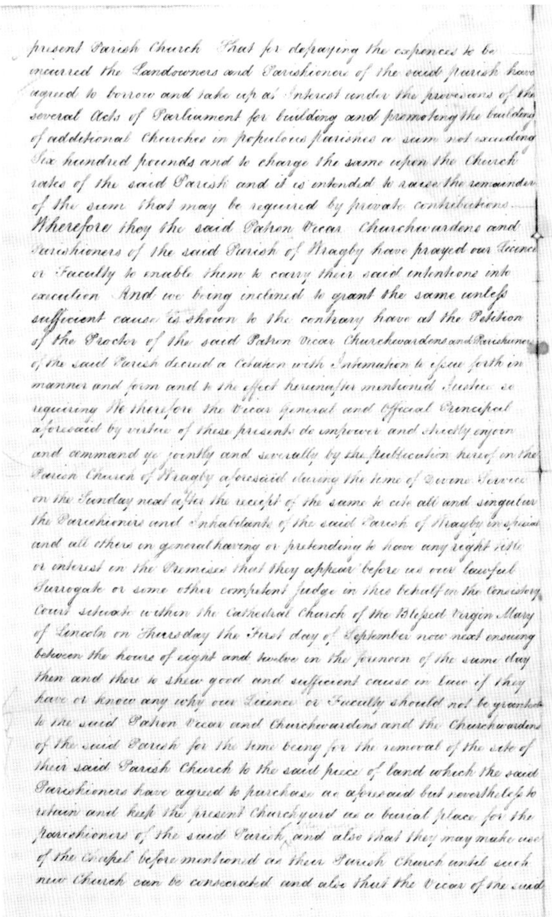

Parish and his Curate may be allowed to read Morning and Evening prayer and to preach and administer the Sacrament to the said Parishioners in the said Chapel and perform all other Offices belonging to the duty of a Minister according to the Liturgy of the Church of England and the rights and ceremonies thereof And further to do and receive as unto Law and Justice shall appertain under pain of the Law and contempt thereof And moreover that ye intimate or cause to be intimated to those so to be cited to whom by the Tenor of these Presents we do hereby intimate that if they some or one of them do not appear at the time and place aforesaid or appearing do not shew good and sufficient cause to the contrary We our Surrogate or some other competent Judge in this behalf do intend and will proceed to grant our Licence or Faculty to the said Patron Vicar and Churchwardens for the purposes aforesaid their absence or contumacy in anywise notwithstanding And what ye shall do in the premises ye shall duly certify us our lawful Surrogate or some other competent Judge in this behalf together with these presents Dated the twenty sixth day of August in the year of our Lord one thousand eight hundred and thirty six —

Geo Swan
Proctor

This Citation with Intimation was read in the Parish church of Rugby aforesaid on Sunday the 28th day of August 1836 during the time of Divine Service —

By me CWhichcote Vicar

Page 3 of the Permission

Edmund Turnor had given the land for the new church and once permission was granted the new church was built. It was completed in 1838 at a cost of £3500, of which £1000 was levied on the parishioners with the remainder given by the patron, the incumbent and the rest of the Turnor family.

The church, designed by William Adams Nicholson of Lincoln, was described as *'a beautiful Norman Gothic building of white bricks and stone dressings, consisting of a chancel, large nave and a high square pinnacled tower which contains a clock and six bells'*. It had *'450 sittings and a good organ, a gift of the Rev. Christopher Turnor. The east window is of stained glass, by Wailes, and represents the Royal Arms of the Bishops of Lincoln and those of the Turnor, Foulis and Whichcote families'*. Unfortunately one of the windows was blown out during WWII. The church register dates from 1567.

It was necessary to restore the church in 1897 at a cost of £530 after which it only had 330 sittings. The church had a new roof in 1908 and further restored at a cost of £300.

The remaining stained glass windows in All Saints Church

Today, apart from its ecclesiastical role, the church is a centre for community activities. The vicar, Rev. Mark Holden, has organised concerts and coffee mornings in the church as well as Bright Sparks which was started in 1999. It is a group, for the under fives and their parents/carers which aim to provide an introduction to the children in arts, crafts and music. They meet once a week and all are welcome.

The vicar also organises the annul Summer Fete which attracts large numbers from the community and surrounding area. He also works hand in hand with the Methodist Minister with 'Churches Together'.

Although, nation wide, it would seem that religion plays a lesser role in the community the church of All Saints is still very much at the centre of Wragby's community.

The Church Bells

A crisis hit the bells of All Saints Church in 1972 when substantial repairs were required. As nothing had been done to the bells or belfry since 1890, Taylor's of Loughborough carried out a survey of the peal. The survey revealed that everything, except the bells, needed replacing. The old wood frame had woodworm and would have to be replaced with a metal frame; all the bells needed turning and would then have to be retuned so that they would be in correct tune with one another. The bells would also have to be fitted with metal headstocks and placed on ball bearings and the new frame would have to rest on girders grouted into the tower. All in all it was an enormous task with the initial estimate being around £2500.

The work was eventually carried out and the bells were welcomed home in May 1974. However, inflation had caused the final bill to be in the region of £3500. £3000 had been raised by the time the bells had been re-installed and the remainder was raised during the rest of the year.

A brief history of the bells:

Sir Edmund Turnor brought bells 3, 4 and 5 to Wragby from Kirmond in 1697 and 3 new bells were made at that time bringing the peal to six. In 1838 the bells were transferred from the old Church (Cemetery Road) to the new church. Although 3 of the bells were cast in 1697 they are still considered to be 'new'. In 1890 the bells were shipped to Messrs. John Warner & Sons of London for the largest bell and the Tenor to be recast and all the bells retuned.

Bell No.1 – This bell (treble) was cast in 1697 by William Noone of Nottingham, who was a founder from 1678 to 1731. The bell has the inscription:

TEMPORE　W STEPHENSON　E T　F WELLS　1697

Bell No.2 – Cast in 1697 by William Noone of Nottingham as was the treble. Heavier than the treble, it measures 28 ½ " and has an inscription which reads:

GOD　SAVE　HIS　CHVRCH　1697

This bell was also the second bell of the Peal in the old church. It is said that this bell had a particular habit of "going badly" and "doing funny things" causing anxious moments for all.

Bell No.3 – Originally cast by Henry Oldfield of Nottingham, Bell Founder 1590-1620 and recast by John Warner in 1890. Inscribed on the bell are the words:

'"JESVS BE OVRE SPEDE" – RECAST BY JOHN WARNER & SONS LONDON 1890

HENRY BOLLAND – VICAR
E BARRY DENNY }
THOMAS COCKETT }CHURCH WARDENS / 1890'.

According to Mr. Tomas North's book *'The Church Bells of the County and City of Lincoln'* (1882) this bell originally carried the following badges of Henry Oldfield.

Yet in Mr. John Ketteringham's book *'Lincolnshire Bells and Bellfounders'* (2000) they are not mentioned. One can only assume they were lost in the recasting though the inscription remains.

Apparently whoever fitted the original wooden casing around the clock did not have any notion of bell ringing as the casing made ringing this bell very difficult.

Bell No.4 – This bell was thought to have been cast somewhere between 1440 and 1510 in a Nottingham Foundry and has the name "Katerine" and bears a shield with the initials 'R C'. The earliest record of this shield is 1371 and the latest is dated 1512. Its early owners are not known but as it was used for some 150 years it is possible that several of the Nottingham founders could have used it. The bell is one of three, which were brought from Kirmond Church by Sir Edmund Turnor and when you hear the clock strike it is this bell you can hear. The full inscription is below:

KATERINE

Bell No.5 – As the 4th it was made between 1440 and 1510 and bears the Latin inscription "Huius Sci Martini. EPI " which translates to 'St. Martin's Bell'). The bell also carries the sign "R.C." Shield as shown below in the full inscription.

Huius Sci Martini Epi

Bell No.6 – As the 3rd this was recast in 1890 by John Warner & Sons of London and also carried the same inscription. However, before it was recast it carried the inscription 'ALL GLORY BEE TO GOD ON HIGH 1697'.

When the bell tower was refurbished to accommodate the new bell frame and girders, it lowered the ceiling of the bell-ringing chamber and gave a very short draught, which resulted in an unsatisfactory ringing of the bells. For nearly 30 years nothing was done, despite frequent mentions from the bell ringers themselves. Finally, with the arrival of the present Vicar, Rev. Mark Holden, things took a turn for the better. Plans were drawn up and fundraising commenced. It was thought practicable that no work should be undertaken until sufficient funds were in place.

Funding for the work was entertaining and varied ranging from cheese and wine evenings to a talk by a member of numerous Antarctic Expeditions. With the very generous support of various sponsors a healthy sum was raised to facilitate the work.

The floor of the bell-ringing chamber has been lowered thereby creating a longer draught. The dangerous old staircase was removed and replaced with a new one and various other works have been carried out. The work started in 2003 and was completed in 2004. All Saints Church can now boast one of the most comfortable bell ringing chambers around and without question one of the safest. Thanks go to all those whose hard work has made this possible and a special mention of Mr. Jim Sutherland, who has persevered and cajoled to get the refurbishment completed.

It is also worth noting that, according to Thomas North's book previously mentioned, in days gone by Wragby Church used to ring the following bells.

The Sermon Bell (Tenor) – Rung after the chiming when a sermon was to be preached.

The Passing Bell – Rung at funerals in such a way as to denote who was being interred (i.e. thrice three tolls for an adult and thrice two for a child regardless of sex. Some tolls also denoted the sex of the deceased.)

Shrive Bell (Pancake Bell) – Rung on Shrove Tuesday at 11 o'clock in the morning.

Mumping Day (St. Thomas' Day) – Tenor bell rung to summon the poor to receive a dole of bread and meat provided by the Churchwardens.

Fire Bell – Special bell rung in case of fire.

Gunpowder Plot – 'Merry Peals' rung to commemorate the discovery of this Plot.

One wonders why they stopped.

Methodist Church

Wesleyan Church

1808 saw the building of the Wesleyan Church in Church Street, its present location. The cost of the land, and building was about £300. Owing to an increased congregation the Church was enlarged, the roof raised and a gallery added. Further improvements were made in 1838. A transept was added to the old Church in 1858-59.

In 1890. as the condition of the Church was causing concern, it was considered necessary to carry out further repairs. At a meeting of the trustees the decision was to *'spend as little as possible on repairs and prepare a scheme for enlargement and renovation'*. Fundraising began towards this end, but in 1894 a decision was made to demolish the Church and build a new one. Mr. Edmund Turnor offered the extra land required and to donate to the scheme. Demolition commenced 5th March 1894.

The stone laying for the new Church took place on 12th April 1894 and the Church opened 6th September that year. It was built to accommodate a congregation of 220.

Old Wesleyan Church

In 1908 some renovation work was carried out and plans set in hand for a new organ, which was installed in December 1912. However, this organ was not thought good enough and it was considered *'helpful to our Sunday services if a better instrument of music could be obtained for public worship.'* The trustees were entrusted to enquire into the purchase of a pipe organ.

This instrument was to be a memorial to all those who lost their lives in the Great War and a brass plaque, with 13 names inscribed, was fitted to the organ.

New Methodist Church

The official opening was February 23rd 1921. Four further names were added as a memorial to those who died in the Second World War. The annual service of Remembrance is held outside the Church every year, when a wreath of poppies is hung on the front door.

The Church is still a centre of worship in Wragby, working closely with the Anglican Church. An Ecumenical Sunday School for the children of Wragby was held there until 1992, and many community functions still take place there. As with All Saints, the Church is a vital part of community life.

Pentecostal Church

In the past there used to be a Pentecostal Church situated on the Lincoln Road where Smithy's Yard is now. We know it was run by Mr. Beech, a signalman at Wragby station, but apart from that not a lot is known about the church or why its congregation declined or when. The picture below was taken in the late sixties and as you can see it was in a total state of disrepair.

Old Pentecostal Church c.1968

Church News by Amanda Wells - 17th July 1964
Last Sunday it was Flower Sunday at church. There were a lot of people. We took flowers and plants and got a book at the end. On Wednesday Mr. Bones blew the whistle and told us that the Sunday School trip was on the 18th August. It is 7/- for grown-ups, 3/6 for young children. Baby brothers and sisters will have to pay 3/6 if they take a seat.

PRAYER TO POLITICS
(Local Governance)

The Parish Clerk

The post of Parish Clerk is one of the most ancient of the lay parish positions. Originally the Parish Clerk was in minor orders, primarily concerned with assisting the parish priest in the services of the parish church and occasionally, in some places, with the education of children. He would lead the singing and the responses of the congregation and also sprinkle 'holy water'.

However, his role changed after the Reformation and the Parish Clerk became more obviously a lay person, say, a parochial officer.

**Edward Orpin
The Parish Clerk
by Thomas Gainsborough**

Parish Clerks of the City of London were registration officers and completed 'Bills of Mortality'. After the returns had been made to those in authority, the Clerks were allowed to sell copies in order to raise money.

Peter Hampson Ditchfield describes his book *The Parish Clerk* (1907) as follows: "*this book comprises recollections of their quaint ways, their curious manners and customs*", and the following extract by The Rev. Canon Hemmans, contained in the book, is of direct relevance to Wragby.

The Rev. Canon Hemmans told of his reminiscences of Thomas Evison, parish clerk of Wragby, Lincolnshire, who died in 1865, aged 82 years. He spoke of him as "*a dear old friend, for whom I had a profound regard, and to whom I was grateful for much help during my noviciate at my first and only curacy*".

Thomas Evison was a shoemaker, and in his early years a great pot-house orator. Settled on his regular corner seat in the Red Lion, he would be seen each evening smoking his pipe and laying down the law in the character of the village oracle. He must have had some determination and force of character, as one evening he laid down his pipe on the hob and said, "I'll smoke no more". He also retired from his corner seat at the inn, but he was true to his political opinions, and remained an ardent Radical to the last. This action showed some courage, as almost all the parish belonged to the squire, who was a strong Tory of the old school.

Canon Hemmans was curate of Wragby with the Rev. G.B. Yard, from 1851 to 1860. Rev. Yard was a High Churchman, a personal friend of Manning, the Wilberforces, R. Sibthorpe, and Keble, and when expounding then unaccustomed and forgotten truths, he found the clerk a most intelligent and attentive listener. Evison used to attend the daily services, except the Wednesday and Friday Litany, as they were too short for him.

It was during the vicar's absence that Canon Hemmans, who was then a deacon, found the clerk a most reliable adviser and instructor in Lincolnshire customs, words and ways of thought. On one occasion he was privately baptizing a child, named Thirza, which he did not recognise as a Bible name. He consulted Evison, who said, *"Oh, yes, it is so; it's the name of Abel's wife"*. The next day Evison bought a book, *Gesner's Death of Abel*, a translation of some Swedish or German work. This is not an uncommon book, and the clerk said the people believed it was as true as the Bible, because it claimed to be about Bible characters.

Evison was an avid reader of newspapers, which were much fewer in his day, and studied diligently the sermons reported in the local Press. He was much puzzled by the reference to 'the leg end' of the story of the raising of Lazarus in a sermon preached by the Bishop of London. A reference to Bailey's Dictionary and the finding of the word 'legend' made matters clear. Of course, he miscalled words. During the Russian War he told Mr. Hemmans that we were not fighting for 'territorial possessions', and he always read 'Moabites and Hungarians' in his rendering of the sixth verse of the 83rd Psalm instead of 'Moab and Hagrites'.

After the resignation of Rev. Yard in 1859, a Low Churchman was appointed, who restored the use of the black gown. Mr. Hemmans had to preach in the evening of the first Sunday, and was undecided whether he ought to continue to use the surplice. He consulted Evison, whose brave advice was, *"Stick to your colours"*.

The clerk stuck stoutly to his Radical principles, and one day went to Lincoln to take part in a contested election. On the following Sunday the vicar spoke of 'the filthy stream of politics'. Although a man of senior years, Evison was rather moved by this, and said afterwards, *"Well, I am not too old to learn"*. Though staunch to his own principles, he was evidently considerate towards the opinions of others. He used to keep a pony and gig, and his foreman, Solomon Bingham, was a local preacher. When inclement weather prevailed on a Sunday morning the kind old clerk would say: *"Well, Solomon, where are you going to seminate your schism to-day? You may have my trap."* Canon Hemmans retains a very affectionate regard for the memory of the old clerk.

In concluding his book, Peter H Ditchfield reflects on the passing of the parish clerk. *"For a thousand years he has held an important position in our churches. We have seen him robed in his ancient dignity, a zealous and honoured official, without whose aid the services of the Church could scarcely have been carried on. In post-Reformation times he continued his career without losing his rank or status, his dignity or usefulness. We have seen him the life and mainstay of the village music, the instructor of young clerics, the upholder of ancient customs and old-established usage. We have regretted the decay in his education, his irreverence and absurdities, and have amused ourselves with the stories of his quaint ways and strange eccentricities.*

His unseemly conduct was the fault of the dullness, deadness, and irreverence of the age in which he lived, rather than of his own personal defects. In spite of all that can be said against him, he was often a very faithful, loyal, pious, and worthy man. His place knows him no more in many churches. We have a black-gowned verger in our towns; a humble temple-sweeper in our villages."

He went on to say that the only civil right still retained by the parish clerk was that the prospectors of new railways are obliged to deposit their plans and maps with him. *"I well remember the indignation of my own parish clerk when, plans for a proposed railway, addressed to the 'Parish Clerk', were delivered by the postman to the Clerk of the Parish Council. It was a wrong that could scarcely be righted."*

Among the most renowned portraits, by Sir Thomas Gainsborough, is that of Edward Orpin, a Parish Clerk. It is said that Gainsborough characterized the stately and refined grace of his figures by his poetic charm. This is most certainly reflected in the portrait of Edward Orpin.

Parish Council

Under the Local Government Act of 1894, Parish Councils were established to take over the management of parochial affairs from Vestries. Vestries had worked well for centuries but its members were not elected and membership was perpetuated by co-option. The formation of Parish Councils brought more democracy and thereafter the Vestry's role was reduced to managing the affairs of the church.

The first meeting of the Wragby Parish Council was held in the Boys School on Tuesday 4th December 1894 at 7p.m. The minutes read:

Mr. J.H. Holmes having briefly explained how the meeting was to be conducted, Dr. E. Barry Denny was elected Chairman at 7.15p.m.

The Chairman made a few remarks expressing a hope that the Parish Council would be elected without putting the Parish to the expense of a poll. The nomination papers were then handed in; the following fourteen candidates were nominated:-

Candidate	Proposer	Seconder
Hill Robert	Dove W.H.	Broxholme Peter
Holmes George	Bratley Benj.	Wright W.O.
Bolland the Rev. H.	Dobson Martin	Fanthorpe W.
Fanthorpe Wm.	Berry W.	Bratley
Weightman John	Mawer H.	Whitley C.
Bratley Amos	Johnson J.B.	Sutton E.H.
Whitely C.	Major J.W.	Hill R.
Mawer Henry	Wieghtman J.	Major J.W.
Wright W.O.	Broxholme P.	Whitely C.
Gaunt Charles	Johnson J.B.	Kendal M.
Phillipson Charles	Sutton W.H.	Weightman M.
Major J.W.	Wright W.O.	Johnson W.
Sharpe George	Atkinson W.G.	Sutton W.H.
Weightman Wm	Kendal M.	Sutton W.H.

A show of hands was then taken with the result that at 8.15p.m. the eight first named candidates were declared to be elected if a poll was not demanded. One elector demanded a poll but subsequently withdrew his demand and at 8.40p.m. Dr. Denny declared the Meeting closed.

Signed - E. Barry Denny, Chairman

Much business has been conducted since 1894 and most of the records, up to 1992, have been lodged in the Lincoln Archives for anyone wishing to research particular historical records. However, it is interesting to reflect on but a few of the problems, initiatives and achievements over the past 100 years, some of which persist to this day.

In May 1895, some six months after the Parish Council was formed, four gentlemen, not named, were elected to look into footpaths at the end of the allotments and the School Committee asked the Parish Council for 5 shillings to cover the cost of a fire and lights for meetings. In December the Parish Clerk complained to the School Committee that there was **no** fire **and** the lamp had not been trimmed, reminding the School Committee that the Council did pay 5 shillings for this service.

Ten years on there was an outbreak of Typhoid and Diphtheria and the Parish Council met with Christopher Turnor, who agreed to have the wells analysed and check the connections to the sewers. The First World War came and went, although in 1918 concern was expressed about the lack of a meat supply for Wragby and neighbourhood.

In 1935 the Council was requested to look into Street Lighting, Speed Limits, Fire Ponds and Footpaths but by the outbreak of the Second World War progress on the supply of electricity was suspended by the Mid-Lincs Electricity Supply Company due to the hostilities.

Were you aware that in the 1960's the Parish Council arranged, and paid for, the installation of additional street lighting utilising old existing electric poles? The County Council was responsible for Mill View before the District Council took over all responsibility. At one time the Market Place was lit from a generator in Holmes yard, behind the Ivy Club.

The 1971 records make mention for Silver Street to be one-way and a pedestrian crossing on Horncastle Road/Cemetery Road. It was in 1973 that the Parish Council's request for a pedestrian crossing was turned down and to this day Silver Street is still two-way, albeit there is now no right turn onto the A158.

Wragby had identified a need for public toilets in 1979. However, the response from the Department of Environmental Health, ELDC considered sufficient toilet facilities were available at the pubs and eating places. Needless to say we now have the toilets.

A complaint was made by Transporters that they could not find Panton Grange in Panton, and approached the Parish Council. A Council Initiative resulted in the Boundary Commission arranging to alter the Wragby Parish Boundary so that Panton Grange on Wire Hill Lane be incorporated into the Parish of Wragby.

Perhaps the most controversial set of the Parish Council initiatives, for many years, was the re-routing of the road, which ran alongside the present Co-op and fish bar, to join the A158 to the Bardney Road; the installation of traffic lights and a pedestrian crossing. There were many objections to the proposals and sadly, like today, it took a fatality before the proposals were accepted.

It will come as no surprise that there have been many changes of roles and responsibilities for Parish Councils over the past 100 years and no doubt further changes will come about in the future. In some small way the salary of the Clerk to the Parish Council reflects these changes in responsibility. In 1895 the Clerk was paid £12 per annum and in 2007 the post was advertised at £7.85 per hour for 42.5 hrs per month, with computer and other equipment provided. Until 1959 all Minutes were handwritten script of different styles reflecting the changes of Clerk, thereafter the Minutes were typed.

The Parish Council currently comprises nine Councillors and the Clerk to the Parish Council. Each of the Councillors are appointed to various areas of responsibility, for example, Risk Assessment, Health & Safety, Cemeteries and Finance. They also attend meetings of other bodies as the council representative.

On the initiative of the Parish Council, in September 2005, a Steering Group was formed to produce The Wragby Parish Plan. The Plan came to fruition in July 2007 and was adopted by the Parish Council. An abridged edition was delivered to every household in Wragby and is aptly described as a Plan 'By the People for the People'.

As part of the action plan to improve communication, the Parish Council has now set up a web site and issued its first Newsletter, which will be published on a four monthly basis.

The Parish Council, in its support of local groups, continues to allocate small grants to deserving causes in Wragby. The present Chairman is Councillor Mrs. June Elborn.

PROMINENT PERSONALITIES

Hugh Bourn

Hugh Bourn lived in a thatched cottage in Holton cum Beckering for seven years before moving to Wragby and it was while in Holton, that he married Monica. He is quite proud of the fact that he rose early on his wedding day, dug a trench, laid a chain of glazed drain and was still on time for his wedding at 2.30 that afternoon.

At that time he farmed 57 acres of land, running some 60 breeding pigs on land which is now covered by the Bridal Way and Ropewalk development. The pigs had to be walked over Silver Street to the pig yard situated where two houses, built by Edward Bourn and his wife Bridget in 2001, now stand. When they were about nine years old his other two sons, Wallace and Christopher, helped with injections etc., in the pig yard. Some 1200 pigs a year were reared there.

150 years ago the yard was the site of a sawmill and wooden hut where the saw millers had their meals. Edward Robinson bought the sawmill and converted it into a milking parlour. For 30 years cows were walked up and down Silver Street twice a day from a field over Louth Road to the parlour for milking. The state of the road can be imagined and it acquired an unflattering local name!

When Hugh Bourn demolished the parlour and hut to create the pig yard he decided to leave the hut fireplace standing and it can still be seen built into a wall.

Hugh Bourn with his Potato Pickers in 1953

In addition to the pigs he rented land from about 15 farmers in the area to grow pulling peas, and up to 300 people from all over North Lincolnshire were employed for about six weeks at harvest time. Ted Bell was the haulier, taking nets of peas to market and Hugh Bourn himself also delivered peas to Nottingham Market, returning for another load and took that to Sheffield before returning home for two to three hours well earned sleep.

It was a suggestion from Monica that started the building enterprise, detailed elsewhere in this book, to help supplement the income from farming. By now the family were living in Wragby, where they have lived for 42 years.

Hugh Bourn recalls that in the past he had to cycle to Legsby with a harrow on his shoulder to get it repaired, a feat which caused some injury because of the weight involved. He also recalled another test of his strength when he hoisted a sack on his back on which Cecil Pycroft then sat, a total weight of 42 stone or about a quarter of a ton.

Now in his seventies, Hugh Bourn, a prominent member of the community, is proud of what he has achieved and he still has one of the first products from Wragby Plastics, an ashtray bearing the statement *'Enjoy yourself it's later than you think',* a sobering thought in the present anti-smoking climate.

Hugh Bourn with his Pigs

Tom Shepherd

(Timely Tom)

Born and raised in East Barkwith, Tom Shepherd came to Wragby in 1932 at the age of 14 when he left school to work for Mr. Rutland. He joined Holmes of Wragby eight years later and stayed with them for 29 years. He then took full time employment at the newly built school in Silver Street, as caretaker, where he stayed for 14 years until he retired aged 65. Tom then became caretaker of the new Town Hall on a part time basis. That was in the days when there was only the main hall with cloakrooms and a tiny kitchen.

Tom winding the clock

This has now become the passage to the annexe and Tom's duties grew with the building, which was extended and finally completed in 1974.

One of Tom's other duties was church warden, caretaker and cleaner. He took over from Mr. Ernest Saggers in 1952 and continued throughout. As caretaker it was his duty to climb 36 steps to wind the church clock every Saturday morning. Although he relinquished the caretaking duties, after oil fired heating was installed, he continued to wind the clock, thus helping to keep the community on time.

Mr David Taylor

There have been several boot and Shoemakers in Wragby over the centuries, the most famous probably being Thomas Evison. From 1792 to the early 1900's there have been two or three at a time listed in the Directories, proving that Wragby was, indeed, an affluent society. However the last, but not least remembered, is David Taylor.

Mr. Taylor started out in the 1930's and every Thursday he would cycle to East Barkwith to spend a day in a small workshop at the rear of Mr. Penrose's post office and grocery shop. Local resident Mrs. Don Tindall recollects taking family shoes to Mr. Taylor in 1936 for repairs. Mr. Taylor sold new boots and shoes and did the usual repairs from his shop on the East side of Market Place, which is now the Country Hair salon.

Mr. Taylor was also a postman delivering mail in Wragby in the mornings, leaving the rest of the day to repair boots and shoes. His shop was also a gossip corner for the men of the village and if you wanted a bet on a horse Mr. Taylor could organise a flutter. Mr. Taylor retired from his shop in the 1970's but carried on repairing shoes and boots, in his garden shed in Cemetery Road, for a few more years.

David Taylor in his Shop - 1965

George Arthur Kilmister 1899 – 1967

Affectionally know as George Arthur or GA, George was born in Woodhall Spa. His Father died when he was three years old leaving his mother, Maria, to raise both George and his sister, Dorothy, single handed. George served in the First World War at Ypres in France, in the trenches, being one of the few who came back after the war.

George did not come from farming stock, he worked as a part-time postman. On one of his rounds he was bitten by a farmer's dog and his trousers were ripped. The farmer, Mr. Hansard, said to him *"It's not a new pair of trousers you want lad – it's a better job"* and offered him a job on his farm, which George took.

In 1926 he was shown round his first farm at Holme Hill, Wragby – courageously, but with much uncertainty, he got his foot on the lowest rung of the farming ladder by renting this small farm. He dared to ask the bank for an overdraft of £20, which was refused, but George persevered and rented the farm. The secret of his success was that he saw farming as a whole, with both its challenges and opportunities.

George was happily married to Marjorie Brothwell, daughter of the local Saddler from Bardney Road, whose shop is now the cottage known as Briar Patch. Marjorie was always a great support throughout his life. George and Marjorie had a son, Steven, and a daughter, Pat. The family eventually moved to Bardney Road Farm, which they rented. Eventually George bought Barn Farm and also, in partnership with Henry Shuttleworth, bought White Lion Farm in Wragby. On his death he owned 600 acres of land around Wragby and was farming a total of 700 acres. His son, Steven, farmed the land until he also died of cancer. Most of the land was then sold.

In Wragby itself, George was the cornerstone of local life, touching every branch of activity, from Parish Council to being the first leader of the Young Farmers Club (YFC). His work with the YFC extended over many years, bringing out his qualities of leadership to the full and the extent to which he participated, showed his enthusiasm at its best. When his interest was aroused, you saw his eyes open wide followed by the contagious smile, that won him so many friends.

There is a plaque in memory of George Arthur in the Town Hall, in appreciation of the work he did for the community. He was primarily responsible for the building of the Town Hall and he worked so hard

George Kilmister with Mrs. S. Bradshaw and Mrs. H. Shuttleworth

through the building phase and to get the Hall up and running when it was completed. Marjorie was always in the background, working tirelessly to support George, baking and serving teas etc., at local events.

George was Governor of Riseholme Agricultural College for many years, Chairman of the Lindsey Milk Committee and served on many other councils and committees. He was serving on the Lincolnshire Show Committee which made the decision to set up the permanent Lincolnshire Showground.

George gave the community of Wragby, the land for the new Cemetery in the Rout Yards and was sadly the first to be buried there after a long battle with cancer.

One remembers George for his exuberance, spirit and his quiet confidence. When days were dark, his helpfulness to all around and his quiet assurance in leadership shone through. He would always famously say *"Boys, it can be done!"*

Leslie Leighton Thorne

Leslie was born in 1923 in the small cottage next to the Methodist Church. His unusual second name comes from his grandmother, Catherine Leighton.

He went to Wragby School, where the teachers were Miss O'Rourke, Mrs. Skipworth and Mr. A.W. Mumby. He failed the final 11 plus, as did everyone in the area. There was just the one place at Horncastle Grammar School – a very sore point with Mr. Mumby.

Leslie left school at 14 and started work for his father Edgar. Edgar was a hard taskmaster but Leslie's mother, Sarah (many people called her Sissie as she was the first girl in the Rowson family – after six boys!), was a very kind lady and protected her youngest son.

In 1942 he was called up and joined REME. He worked on tanks at Catterick, where he was promoted to Craftsman and then Lance Corporal. He was posted to North Africa where he worked on motorbikes and Italy, where the workshop reconditioned 150 Ford V8 engines each day. He was given a class B (bee?) release in May 1946 and flown home, in a Dakota, to return to work with his ailing father in an important industry - beekeeping.

Edgar trained Leslie in painting, decorating, signwriting and, of course, beekeeping. The business needed all those skills to make a living and Leslie can remember working on many of the big houses in Wragby. Then, Leslie got his first big break. Mr. A.B. Dove (no Christian names used in the late 1940's) asked him to build him a bungalow. Leslie had never laid a brick in his life but Mr. Dove said *"Your Dad's always done my work and I trust you"*.

After many attempts by Archie Stephenson, of Langton Hill, to play matchmaker, Leslie was finally introduced to Joan Maddison, of Bardney, at a Bardney Dairies Sunday School Anniversary. They married in 1950 and Leslie built a two-storey extension on the side of his parents' house. They had two daughters and soon Joan joined him in the business. She was a trained typist and had worked at Bardney Sugar Beet factory before her marriage. She was also the cover girl for the first beet factory magazine!

From a boy, Leslie was interested in Magic Lanterns. When Rev. Fox moved from the Vicarage, (about 1957) a sign outside said 'Many items for Sale'. In he went and found a 3.5mm cine camera, screens, films and all the accessories. He bought it for £5. He really enjoyed using this and soon upgraded to 16mm. He took films of all Wragby events and eventually, in the 1990's, put these together on video. At this time, the Methodist Church organ, which Leslie had played for 65 years, needed an expensive overhaul so he sold these videos to help raise funds for this.

Dick Bones, the local schoolmaster and keen stills photographer, heard that Granada TV in Manchester were looking for a freelance cameraman to cover the Lincoln area. Leslie applied and, after sending them a ten minute film of *"The Brook"*, he got the job. For ten years, he filmed many interesting events for TV; the Queen opening Pelham Bridge in Lincoln, various Prime Ministers, Air Shows, Spalding Flower Parade, train and air crashes and more.

It almost got him into serious trouble one day, when President John Kennedy flew in briefly to Waddington. Leslie went and surreptitiously took film, from outside the base, but he soon had a tap on his shoulder. The film was confiscated and Leslie hit the headlines locally, accused of shooting President Kennedy.

Leslie was a member of the Wax Chandlers Company of London and a freeman of the City of London. For many years he was also the President of Wragby Show & Country Fayre.

Leslie lived in Wragby all his life and in his latter years spent much of the winter in Tenerife. He counted himself lucky to have made his living out of his hobby – beekeeping and continued to look after the bees at the apiary, on the edge of the town, until his untimely death on 13th January 2007.

Leslie Thorne presenting the Ten Cap Catering Shield at Wragby Show

Jim Sutherland

Jim, of 1932 vintage, was born in Nairnshire – no hint of an accent! His father came south, alone, in 1937 to a farm at Walesby, Lincolnshire to carry out the Winter and Spring cultivations for his boss, a Scots farmer. After returning to Scotland he eventually came back to the Walesby farm and settled, with his family, in 1938.

Some years later Jim served his apprenticeship as a barber and, in 1952, started work for a barber in Caistor. It was in 1961 that Jim became aware Mr. I.W. Sutton, hairdresser of Wragby, was considering retirement and Arthur Johnson offered Jim premises to start up his own business as a barber.

Horncastle Rural District Council raised doubts as to whether the premises could be used for business purposes. However, Jim produced 'evidence' and the RDC confirmed he could go ahead, on the proviso that when he started to earn money the rateable value would be assessed. Mr. Sutton retired over the Bank Holiday and Jim opened his business in January 1962, travelling from Walesby on a daily basis. Jim remarked on how kind the people of Wragby had been to him at that time. In particular Mr. & Mrs. Arthur Johnson and Ken Johnson, who had rented him the premises and Mr. Sutton, who handed his stock over saying that he didn't need to pay for at least three months.

In 1963 Jim married Margaret, they settled in Holton Beckering and later that year he was advised that he should consider a part time postman job and get out in the fresh air. To this end he went for a medical, after which Dr. Roe told him that it was the best thing he could do.

Jim Sutherland and his new Post Office van

In the August of that same year, a job as a holiday relief postman became available which he accepted. He was shown the round by Mrs. Bratley, who cycled 19 miles a day delivering the post. In October Jim was offered the position of part-time postman covering Rand, Fullnetby and Bullington. He used a bicycle from Mrs. Humberstone, and later graduated to a moped. The two jobs fitted together well; Postman in the mornings and Barber in the afternoons.

Almost two years later Jim and Margaret moved from Holton Beckering to the old doctors surgery, now the Corn Dolly. On the advice of Arthur Johnson, Margaret started a Drapery and Haberdashery business. Both businesses went well for some years but following a spell of ill health they decided to give up the two businesses and in March 1973 moved to the Gatehouse on Wire Hill Lane. Jim reflects on the fact that they had looked at the Gatehouse, as a potential home, years earlier when it was derelict. He carried on as Postman and spent part of his time selling Betterware products until three years later, when he filled a vacancy for a full time postman which lasted until his retirement in May 1996.

Jim has been ringing bells since the age of ten and started at Wragby when living at Holton Beckering. He graduated to Tower Captain in 1977 when Mr. Fred Cook retired, due to ill health. This skill and interest has taken him all over the UK, ringing at 55 towers in one week. We have all heard the story that bellringers occasionally forget to let go of the rope and are lifted high. Jim says this is somewhat of a myth. In all his years as a bellringer, he has only ever seen this happen once, at Caistor. It was the Bank Manager who suddenly shot up whereupon the other bellringers just laughed and one remarked *"I see the bank rate has just gone up"*!

George Alfred (Bill) Woolgar
(1911 – 1993)

Born in Warsop, Nottinghamshire, George (quite often referred to as Bill) was a police constable in Wragby in the early 1940's before becoming the village newsagent with a shop in the Market Place, now Dhindsa Premier Stores. A café was added to the premises and 'The Barn' became a favourite halfway house for traffic going to and from the coast.

George was noted for his wit and conviviality along with the many kindnesses he performed. He once offered a young lady customer £10 to give up smoking for her own good – which she duly did – and he was the village tobacconist!

He took a great deal of interest in the village and, along with Ron Brothwell, Tommy Lockton and others, did a lot of fundraising towards the building of the Town Hall. This hosted many Saturday night 'hops' and saved young people having to go to Lincoln for weekend entertainment.

George was involved in starting both the Bingo and the '200 Club', both of which are still running. He was also involved with the establishment of the Swimming Pool, the children's playground and personally opened the Dove Park Bowling Green. He always got involved in and promoted the Wragby Summer Fete, which now attracts folk from all over the area.

In the 1970's a local tramp, called Harry, used to frequent houses and shops in Wragby for a few scraps of food. Don Wells at the fish and chip shop would give him a few chips and George a cup or mug of tea. As Harry was always around somebody's door George gave a lorry driver £1 to take Harry to Skegness to get him away for a while, maybe indefinitely. However, true to form Harry was back in Wragby some four hours later. It is thought that the driver may have 'dumped' him in Baumber, probably because his wardrobe was a bit on the strong side.

**George Woolgar in his 'Barn' papershop
Market Place c.1965**

The Brothwell Family

The Brothwell family were saddlers whose workshop was once located in what is now the Ivy Club. The building was bought by George Mawer in the great sale of Wragby in 1917 and became part of the family home 'Ivy House'.

Not to be disconcerted Mr. William Brothwell moved his business further down the Bardney Road to continue his trade.

Brothwell Saddlers Shop pre 1917

The first mention of the Brothwell's is in the 1828 Directory which lists William Brothwell as a Wheelwright. In 1841 William's son, Richard, had joined him in the business and had taken over completely by 1856. Richard and his wife, Mary, had seven children, but only Thomas followed the Wheelwright trade. Son, James became an apprentice Saddler as did Thomas' son, William. When Richard died, in 1851, Mary carried on trading as Mary Brothwell & Sons (Thomas and Grandson William). In 1891 James Brothwell, Saddler, was lodging with his mother, Mary. As there were other wheelwrights listed in Wragby, in those years, one presumes that the change to Saddler was a more profitable one. Mary Brothwell died in 1888 and in 1891 grandson, William had taken over from James, who was now a farmer.

William married Maria and had five children, three girls and two boys. In the photograph below, taken in 1903, the youngest daughter had yet to be born, one girl died as a child and the eldest girl, at the back, was to die in her late teens.

The Brothwell Family in 1903

The boy on the right became Corporal William (Billy) Brothwell who, with Trooper J. Mawer, Sergeant E. Hobbins and Lieutenant Clarke (Vet.), all in the Lincolnshire Yeomanry, survived the 'Mercian' tragedy in November 1915. Only one local died of injuries sustained in the submarine attack. This was Trooper G. H. Ward, son of William and Fanny Ward of Goltho, formerly a pupil of Wragby School and the first of the old pupils to lose their life in the war. He is buried in Le Petit Lac Cemetery in Algeria.

Corporal Wm. (Billy) Brothwell

Both Billy and his brother, Joseph, played in Wragby's football team, when Wragby were Champions! Sadly Billy died in 1930 with both his parents outliving him.

Wragby Champions 1922/23
Billy is back row far right and Joseph middle row far left

William Brothwell died just before the Second World War, ending over 100 years of trade in Wragby. His wife, Maria, died in 1947 and both are buried in the old cemetery. Their granddaughter Ena can remember walking in crocodile fashion behind the coffin from the house all the way to the cemetery. *It is Ena we*

William Brothwell with Clarke Holmes outside the Bardney Road Shop

THE WAR YEARS

1914 – 1918

There is little information about Wragby's involvement in WWI but here we give an insight of one man's experiences. It is especially poignant when at the time of collating information for this publication the spotlight is again on the Middle East.

'It was late afternoon on 1st November 1917 when we rode into Beersheba and watered the horses at Abraham's Wells. The old city had fallen to the Australian Light Horse the previous day and the Turkish grip on Palestine had at last been loosened. The Lincolnshire Yeomanry had spent the previous 12 months advancing slowly over the waterless waste of Sinai and had played its part in two abortive attempts to dislodge the Turks from the stronghold of Gaza.

**Trooper Albert Burrell Dove
Serving in the
Lincolnshire Yeomanry
1914-1918**

On leaving Beersheba the Yeomanry Mounted Division headed North into the land of Canaan but stubborn Turkish rearguard action and shortage of water held up the pursuit. The infantry had taken Gaza and a general advance was ordered. Crossing over westwards to the coast in search of water, we followed the course of the Crusaders path reaching Ramleh and later Lydda (where the tomb of St. George, patron Saint of England, is situated) where a halt was called before the final assault to bring about the capture of Jerusalem was staged. The date was 18th November 1917.

We turned our backs to the sea and struck out eastwards where our Brigade took the path that had seen the Assyrians, Crusaders, Philistines and Greeks and where the Roman Cavalry had turned back in 66 AD. The track got worse and worse and to add to our troubles the winter rains came earlier that expected which fell and fell. Men and horses floundered in the conditions. Because of the quickness of the advance the wheeled transport had been left behind, the men were still in summer dress and there was little food left for men or horses.

It rained incessantly for two days and life was miserable for everyone. All the time we were slowly pressing forward but we desperately needed food and water for the animals and ourselves. Finally we met the supply column at Beth Huron. Never were rations more welcome and for a while, at least, we were able to rest and refresh ourselves. However, our part was not over yet.

On the morning of 28th November we were awakened by heavy rifle fire, the Turks had followed our withdrawal and were counter attacking. We found ourselves in a desperate situation. In response to an urgent appeal for assistance the 7th Mounted Brigade made a forced march and came into action on our exposed flank and the Turks were driven back. They had been shelling our positions with great accuracy and doing a lot of damage amongst the horses of Brigade Artillery but we held on in spite of the problems.

Towards nightfall a company of the Scottish Rifles drew up. They had been sent to our relief and they soon took over the advanced posts between the opposing sides. We could hear the Turks calling to one another in the darkness and an exchange of rifle fire was kept up throughout the night. Despite this, we were able to get some sleep, shielded as we were by the screen of Scottish Infantry.

The next morning more relief came and we were eventually withdrawn to Ekron and so ended our part in the taking of Jerusalem. The city eventually surrendered to General Allenby on 9th December 1917. Later General Allenby at Ekron reviewed us before we handed over our horses in preparation for our transfer to France where we were to be retrained as gunners. In the 12 days our Division had been in the Judean Hills we lost a third of our strength owing to casualties and illness.'

From just this one story the deprivations and struggles our men faced in this war to end wars come alive. Imagine then, if you will, the same conditions spread over the Somme and Ypres and all the other places in the world where battles were fought. It really doesn't bear thinking about and yet our men gladly went to war to fight for our freedom and belief in democracy. It is a wonder any of them came back.

The Lincolnshire Regiment Market Place 1913

For those men of Wragby who did not return memorial plaques in both Churches are engraved with their names:

Charles Barton	Martin Bratley	Luther Bratley
George Frederick Broxholme		Bertram Chapman
Robert William Clarke		George Hubbard
John Benjamin Dobson	Harry Davidson	Charles Thornton
George William Sharpe	Charles Kew	William Wilson

1939 – 1945

Wragby had 254 Air Raid warnings during WWII, the first being on September 4th 1939, the day after War was declared, and the last on April 22nd 1944. The Chief Air Raid Warden was Mr. Frank Seely, who had lived for some years at Gothic House in the Market Place.

According to Frank the greatest density of warnings took place in June 1940 and again in March 1941. Alerts lasted from just a few minutes to several hours and sometimes more than once a night. Fortunately there were no casualties in Wragby itself but five bombs that fell on Walk Farm, Langton on September 5th 1940 killed five animals and other raids brought bombs to Panton, East Barkwith, Hainton, Fullnetby and Benniworth between September 1940 and May 1941. One daylight raider passing low over Wragby was shot down at Baumber on 3rd July 1942.

The Wragby and District Warden's service was well organised and trained when war broke out and gave a dedicated service throughout war. Warnings came via County Control to Gothic House and from there, the wardens in the town were notified and the Mobile First Aid party held in readiness.

The greatest danger came from our own crashed aircraft, both when taking off fully loaded or returning, after operations, to the many bomber stations which surrounded Wragby. Many houses and farmsteads narrowly escaped destruction though several were damaged, fortunately without any loss of life. Wragby had a ringside seat when it came to the hundreds of planes on their way to bomb German towns and it was with mixed feelings that the residents watched this nightly spectacle.

Troops checking Bus - Market Place c.1943

(This picture was taken from a window in the Turnor Arms as photographing the military or installations was forbidden)

As women view things differently from men, the changes that Wragby experienced during this time were perhaps more poignant for the women. Imagine, seeing your young child going off to school with a gas mask box over their shoulder; the young men being called up to War and disappearing from the town. The shock of food rationing, utility clothing, no Church bells and the blackouts; not being able to buy clothes without clothing coupons and items, one by one, no longer available; your every day routines turned upside down. These are the things women saw. Yet they all battled on as best they could. The women also met weekly, to knit a variety of articles for the troops and also to collect salvage which was then sorted in the Vicarage.

It was early in 1940 that Wragby had its first contingent of soldiers stationed in the town - the South Nottinghamshire Hussars. At first they were billeted with residents but in short order army huts appeared and empty rooms and buildings were requisitioned. A Sergeants Mess, Officers Mess and Guard Room appeared, among others, a small garrison town in fact. Apparently when the Hussars left they were escorted to the train by half the population and given a terrific send off.

Following the Hussars were various companies of Royal Engineers and when the 6th Field Park Company Royal Engineers came direct from Dunkirk (hollow eyed, gaunt and clothes held together with string) the full horror of the War hit Wragby between the eyes. The women of Wragby took all the boys to their hearts and mothered them, darning their socks and doing their laundry, but most of all inviting them into their homes.

At this time the Methodist Church Schoolroom had become a soldier's welfare canteen and used by them for meals and fellowship - as an alternative to the local inns. It was run by the W.V.S. and organised by Mrs. Rushworth. She asked for volunteers and drew up a weekly rota comprising women and girls and at least one man to see that order was maintained. The canteen was open each weekday evening from 7pm until 10pm and after the evening service on Sundays. The soldiers, together with the RAF and WAAF personnel, from Wickenby were all keen to avail themselves of the amenities.

After the departure of the Royal Engineers came the Tower Hamlets from the East End of London and then the Royal Artillery. 'Bateman's Folly' was built in the Market Place and barriers appeared on each street.

The Home Guard c.1943
Not all the names are known but included are the following from Left to Right in position:
Front Row: 2-Bill Lowe, 3-Harry Rowson, 4-Tom Shepherd, 5-Mr. Norcross,7-Percy Mawer, 8-Sammy Proctor,
          9-Joe Dixon, 10-Jack Anderson, 11-George Coupland
Middle: 1-Bill Munton, 2-Jack Martin, 3-Alwyn Johnson, 5-Billy Height, 7-Tom Dixon, 8-Jeff Sergeant,
          9-Hubert Tuplin, 10-Ron Potter
Back: 2-Jim Brothwell, 5-Archie Booth, 7-John Ward, 8-Alf Davison, 9-Dave Taylor

The Park and Rout Yards were taken over for exercises and slit trenches were dug. Wragby became almost unrecognisable with manoeuvring tanks and occasional explosions. One such explosion being a mite too big smashed the stained glass window in the Church and the Wragby 'pigs' had gone forever. A new window, in memory of Canon Moore, eventually replaced it.

Wragby also had its equivalent of Dad's Army. The Home Guard was made up of local men and led by Major A.B. Dove, Captain R. Hughes and Lt. P. Mawer. They each took turns watching from the Church tower, although one of their number was found to be too fat to get up the tower, much to the amusement of his companions.

Although the initial reaction of the troops to Wragby was unfavourable to say the least, by the end of their stay they were sorry to leave. So much so that several of them chose their brides from Wragby's girls. The Church parades, at this time' were a splendid sight with the Regular Army, Cadets, Home Guard, Guides, W.V.S. and Civil Defence all involved. The Church was packed. There were also Cinema Shows and Christmas parties for the children.

In 1942 the Royal Engineers Depot in Lincoln was bombed and was subsequently moved to Wragby. A large house was requisitioned and local men, women and girls were pressed into service. It became a common sight to see troops and equipment filling the once peaceful lanes and train loads of ammunition and bombs passing through the station.

During the war years Wragby also had its complement of evacuees, children from Hull, who, no doubt, felt homesick at first, then settled down in the friendly atmosphere of the town. In fact one of their number felt so at home they stayed for many years afterward. Prisoners of War were also in evidence in their odd uniforms, Italian and German; they made a pathetic sight, not at all the monsters the people had been led to believe they were.

With peace in sight, the residents of Wragby wanted to organise something to give their boys and girls a suitable welcome home and on 8th March 1945, 62 parishioners attended a Public Meeting in the Old Grammar School to discuss this. It was decided that all money raised should be divided equally between all those eligible and that Langton and Goltho should be invited to join in the effort. A target of £1000 was agreed and that a 'Home Coming Week' would be held during the week commencing Monday 21st May.

The special week went ahead with events held every day - Garden Fete, Baby Show, Fancy Dress, Band Concert, Domino and Whist Drives and an auction. A subscription List was also opened. Two people, Ernest Wright and Trot Weightman, were foremost in these efforts. One brilliant idea they had was the acquisition of a barrel organ which they trundled round playing tunes and collecting funds of £18. By July £871 had been raised and by October the target had been passed. The W.V.S. made a contribution of £75 which came from their work catering for the troops in the canteen. On 28th January 1946, another Public Meeting was held and arrangements were made for the distribution of the fund, which took place on 16th March. The presentations were made by Commander J.W. Maitland, M.P. and the sum of £15 16s 6d was given to each of the 69 men and women (or their representatives) in gratitude for their services.

At this point we would like to make tribute to those who fought on our behalf. Unfortunately we do not know all of them but of those we do know we can mention. Harry Thorne, first reported missing in Italy, then as a prisoner of war, from where he escaped several times, eventually returning home safely. Jack Burnett who was a prisoner of war in Japan for four years. Maurice Taylor and Stanley Burnett both of whom were badly wounded on D-Day 1944. May Cook who was killed in a NAAFI in Lincoln. Ben Weightman DFC, lost on a Path finder reconnaissance and Lenny Dixon, killed as he set foot on Normandy, D-Day 1944.

The following names were added to the Memorial plaques in both Churches:

Joseph Kenneth Button   **Leonard Alfred Dixon**
John Bentley Weightman DFC   **Beatrice May Cook**

In later years it was decided to include the name of **Clifford Havercroft** on the memorial as it was thought that although he was not directly killed during the fighting, he sustained such grave injuries which subsequently led to his suicide shortly after peace was declared.

To all those who fought in both World Wars for our freedom and democracy we, the children of the future, thank you.

Bateman's Folly

Wragby Fort was erected in 1940, made of concrete and apparently built by Army Sergeant Bateman, with a Company of Royal Engineers, hence the name. It was 20 feet high and 12 feet wide having three levels with access being from an iron ladder in the corner of the ground floor. All levels had weapon sites and it stood in the middle of the Market Place so that it covered all four road junctions. A bren gun mounting was situated at the top. Needless to say it was never used for the purpose of defence. However, it was used as a shelter by the night fire watchers in bad weather and who knows what else!

After the war the problem of demolition was resolved by an explosives expert from Grasby Quarry. He worked downwards by drilling holes and inserting charges. He would then run around the corner leading to the Red Lion yard and blow his whistle. Upon hearing this the shop keepers would protect their windows with corrugated iron sheets, all traffic would be halted and when all safe the charges would be detonated. Debris would fly in all directions in greater or lesser amounts, owing to the variable strength of the structure, until the site was cleared and the Market Place restored.

Wragby Fort both in its prime and part demolished

Post War Housing

Family housing was a problem for some in the post war years as highlighted by an article in the Lincolnshire Echo in 1954.

The picture shows a portion of what was then known as the 'Adam & Eve' housing site with Mrs. Hewerdine brushing her front step.

Around 1949 Mr. Hewerdine had apparently been told to leave his previous rundown dwelling, through no fault of his own, by the Ministry of Health. The Rural Council Housing Committee then told him to take his family to the 'Adam & Eve' housing site. Thinking they were going to a pleasant, romantic sounding estate, they cheerfully departed Ranby. Imagine their shock and horror at finding their new home was a small ex-army hut with three inner partitions. With no other prospects they had to move in. Mr. Hewerdine again approached the Housing Committee in Horncastle and was told there was no need to be unduly perturbed as it was only temporary.

Five years later Mr. Hewerdine, his wife and three children were still living there, longingly looking at the new housing estate that was being built about 100 yards away. Will we be one of the lucky ones and get a new house?, they ask themselves. *We wonder if they did.*

Army Cadet Force

The Wragby Platoon was part of the Horncastle Company of the Lincolnshire Regiment and formed in 1942/43. The Platoon initially had their headquarters in the Reading Room, which was situated above the shops in the Market Place, and comprised approximately 20 in number. One of the cadets, Jack Potter, rose to the rank of Lieutenant during the life of the platoon which finally disbanded in 1957.

Route marches, drills, weapon training and one week camps were the norm. It is reported that during one of the camps the regular officers challenged the cadet officers to a shooting competition - needless to say the cadet officers won. The regulars did not realise the farming background of the cadet officers and that many had been shooting from an early age.

Wragby Army Cadets - 1945
Back Row L-R: Jack Baxter, Geoff Dixon, Sid Jollands, Roy Shuttleworth, Colin Warton
Middle Row: Ray Rounce, Joe Wilkinson, Malcolm Applewhite, Capt. Turnbull, Stan Grundy,
Jack Dixon, Norman Warner
Front Row: Ray Lincoln, Alf Shaw

Wragby A.T.C. By C. Andrew - 9th October 1964
Last Sunday daddy took the A.T.C. Boys gliding at Kirton Lindsey. Some of the boys helped with the gliders and they all went up three or four times. One boy was up for two hours.

AGRICULTURE

Farming

Farming was the main source of employment for Wragby, each worker having his own tied cottage, with pig sty and garden, which would provide much of the food for the family. Farms would have a variety of animals; pigs, chickens, sheep, beef and dairy cattle. Apart from grassland the chief crops were wheat, beans, barley and oats, in fact what is known as mixed farming.

Harvesting Mangolds in a soggy field - 1912
George Taylor, Charles Burman. Henry Clark and George Waddingham

In addition to men employed on the land, Wragby had several trades allied to farming. Blacksmiths would not only shoe farm horses but also mend and sometimes make farm implements. Saddlers repaired the horses' harness and in harvest, stitched up and mended binder canvass. The timber yard produced gates, fencing hurdles and tumbrels, while the rope maker, from which the name Rope Walk is taken, produced binder twine, sheep nets and covers for stacks.

Butchers had their own slaughter houses where locally bought animals would be killed and cut up before being sold in the Wragby shops or delivered locally. Corn merchants and millers bought corn on the shake of a hand and then either cleaned it for seed corn or ground it for animal feed in the mill on Bardney Road. It would then be delivered to local farmers as pig and poultry meal. Auctioneers, valuers and land agents held fairs in May, September and November for cattle, sheep and foals while agricultural engineers repaired farm machinery. Wragby also had a vet, egg merchant, wheelwright and carpenter.

Milk was delivered by tricycle from the dairy. Some residents of Wragby still remember trying to ride the trike, but because the milk was carried on the front, it was difficult to steer and was a job for the expert.

Except for the introduction of sugar beet after the building of the Bardney sugar beet factory in 1929, this pattern of farming continued up to the outbreak of the Second World War.

In the 1930's farming was experiencing very hard times but with the outbreak of war, farmers were urged to produce as much food as possible. Merchant shipping was being sunk by U boats and food was rationed.

It was at this time that farms began to be mechanised. Tractors replaced horses and this meant that larger implements could be used. Many meadows and grasslands were ploughed up and new crops introduced. Flax was grown for fibre. The crops were pulled from the ground, sent to the flax factory where it was processed and the resulting fibres used for parachute harnesses and soldiers' webbing. Peas were grown for drying, either to be sold for human consumption or turned into animal feed.

Mechanisation continued, combine harvesters were introduced and gone were the familiar sights of binders, stooks, corn stacks and threshing engines. Sack driers dried the corn which had been combined, milking machines replaced hand milking and the number of workers on the farms was reduced. The number of ancillary trades also diminished but many of the redundant farm workers found employment in the Plastics factory.

Jack Potter harvesting with a David Brown Tractor and Sail Binder - 1950's

Because of the need for food and the use of bigger machinery, hedgerows were uprooted and sprays were used to control weeds as fallowing was no longer practical. Artificial fertilizers replaced farmyard manure.

The traditional mixed farming was replaced by more specialised farms. Oil seed rape was introduced to produce oil for machinery and cooking. Peas were grown for freezing, the crop being cut and transported by lorry to Grimsby for vining and freezing. Over production has meant that peas are now grown nearer the freezer factories and harvested with huge vining machines so they can be frozen '*as fresh as the day the pod went pop*'.

In the post war years, Mr. Kilmister was seen as a visionary because of his interest in the development of agriculture. He had very high standards of farming and as members of British Seed Growers he and Mr. Shuttleworth grew crops of red and white clover, ryegrass, cocksfoot and timothy on the Wragby farms with the aim of improving the quality of grass leys throughout the country. Improvements in pasture brought improvements in animal production.

It had been a tradition in the Wragby area that Irishmen came annually to help with the sugar beet and corn harvest. During the war prisoners and displaced persons were regularly employed on the farms and there was at least one land girl, working for Mr. Robinson.

In recent years farming has once again undergone great changes. Corn mountains and other surpluses have meant that land has been taken out of cultivation and put into set-aside. Farmers have been encouraged to join the Countryside Stewardship Scheme and many fields now have six metre strips round them while hedgerows are left to grow and only cut twice in five years. Hedgerows that have been uprooted, in the past, are now being replaced and trees planted.

Primrose Hill Farm has a 12,000 free range chicken unit and is also home to a large dairy herd. Machinery has become even larger and combines and drills are now guided by satellite.

Many other changes have occurred. Small holdings have been sold for housing, In fact of all the allied trades once so much a part of Wragby life, not one is left.

Wragby and District Young Farmers Club

The Young Farmers movement nationally had been in existence for some years but it did not reach Lincolnshire until the early 1940's. Mr. George Kilmister, a former member of the National Farmers Union (NFU), approached local farmers and their families to form a club in Wragby. During that summer, with Lancaster bombers droning overhead, many visits were arranged. They included one to the Experimental Station at Kirton, near Boston and one to Bardney Dairies to see two of the first combine harvesters working in a field of wheat. This was then taken to a very slow continuous drier.

It is worth remembering that when the club was formed in 1944, everyone was looking forward to the end of the Second World War. However, numerous people were still appearing before the courts for showing lights during the blackout. The New Years message from the Ministry of Agriculture to farmers and farm workers was *"War is relentless, there can be no ease until the cease fire ends. When the moment comes, agriculture will still have its part, and a very important part, in promoting conditions favourable to a secure and lasting peace. We have raised production to a height never before reached in Britain. Let us now raise the level of efficiency to the same peak, efficiency in crop growing, in livestock production and in farm management, whether the farm is 50 or 100 acres. Then and only then shall we maintain a healthy and well balanced agriculture, for peace may well prove as relentless as war."*

The Young Farmers of 1947

The Young Farmers Club (YFC) was seen as a way of educating young people in the new ideas coming into farming. The first winter programme was planned with activities, such as talks on new machinery, farm records and book keeping. The clubs in the District of Lindsey then decided to form the Lindsey Federation of YFC's to be amalgamated with the National Federation. Competitions were arranged with other county clubs in public speaking and cattle judging. The YFC Rally came next, annually at first and then two each year in the Spring and Autumn, to include seasonal activities such as hedge laying, ploughing, thatching and sheep shearing.

Under Mr. Kilmister's able leadership, the Wragby members recorded considerable successes with many first places at the Rallies and in competitions. The Club has continued to flourish, giving the members the opportunity to participate in activities, which are both social and educational, with the emphasis always on fun. In recent years they have claimed the title of " County Club of the Year " on numerous occasions and for the last five years they have been Rally Champions, after competing with other clubs in exhibitions and working classes.

In 1974, following the re-organisation of local government, The Lincolnshire Federation of YFC's was formed by the amalgamation of the three counties of Lindsey, Kesteven and Holland. The trophies awarded at the county rally each year act as a memento of the former counties. In 1999, celebrations were organised by former members to mark the special occasion in the Federation's history, the first 25 years of Lincolnshire Young Farmers.

During 1994, Wragby Young Farmers arranged their own celebrations to commemorate their fiftieth anniversary, with a reunion at the County Showground. This was a tremendous success and was attended by many former members who enjoyed a happy social evening together. The first club chairman, Ron Potter, was president of the organising committee and Richard Needham was appointed chairman. The commemorative handbook produced, recorded many of the highlights of Wragby YFC over 50 years, and the personalities that contributed to its continuing success.

Farmers and farming generally are currently going through very difficult times but the continuity and success of Wragby and District Young Farmers Club has been assured by the hundreds of young people who have generated a tremendous amount of energy and enthusiasm into its activities for over 60 years. Not all are necessarily connected with agriculture but with every club having the countryside, in all its aspects, as a common theme in their programme.

**Young Farmers Club Members Today
Raising Funds for Charity**

❖❖

Farm News by Patrick Allen - 8th May 1964
This week we have got our drilling done. We put the beet in last. The wheat is sprouting. Most of the farmers have got drilled up. We shall soon roll the barley and the wheat.

INNS & HOSTELRIES

In the past Wragby boasted four Inns/Public Houses serving a population of 700 in 1828. Even today we have two Public Houses, one licensed club and one licensed restaurant which is more than sufficient for a small town/large village; more than most. However, Wragby has always relied on passing trade; people travelling to and from the coast and elsewhere, so one can safely presume that this is the reason they survive.

Little is known about some of the earlier premises, therefore we have had to rely on various Directories and census entries for information. Bearing this in mind we have dealt with the histories of each Inn/Public House individually.

The earliest principal Inns mentioned are in the 1792 Directory, which names the Nag's Head and the White Lion, with Thomas Burrows and John Coney listed as Innkeepers. Unfortunately the Directory doesn't say who kept which Inn! Also listed are Benjamin Harrison and Robert Bell, as victuallers, but again it is unclear whether they are licensed or just provision merchants.

Nag's Head/Turnor Arms

This was the main Coaching Inn throughout the years. You can see from the picture below, which is a copy of a painting, that coaches used to enter via the archway into the yard and the stables beyond. Today the archway has been filled in but you can still see where it was and its size, as the stonework is still there and is, in fact, the front door. It is not as big as you might have expected.

The Nag's Head c.1825

According to Directories and the relevant census' the names of the Innkeepers are listed below with the exception of 1792 as explained above.

1828*	Mary Ketchion (Inn and Posting House)
1835, 1841 and 1861	Joseph Hutchinson (Posting and commercial and Excise Office)
1871, 1872 and 1881	William Brown (Posting and Commercial, Victualler and Farmer)
1885, 1891, 1901 - 1909	Moses Kendall (Family & Commercial Hotel, Vicutaller and Farmer - although in 1871 and 1881 he was a Plumber and Glazier)
1913 and 1919	Joseph Phillipson
1937	Allison Montague Applewhite

The Turnor Arms has recently been refurbished and now includes a restaurant area; the old stables have been turned into living accommodation and a small housing estate has been built in what was once the yard. It lies on the North side of the Market Place and a flush bracket Ordinance Survey Bench Mark No.S0657 is situated just by the new wall, at almost pavement level.

*Somewhere between 1826 and 1835 the name was changed to the Turnor Arms, probably when Mary Ketchion ceased to be the Innkeeper.

White Lion

As can be seen from the copy of a painting below, the White Lion was also a coaching Inn with an archway through to the back. Unfortunately very little is mentioned about the White Lion in the Directories. Entries for 1828 list Philip Turner as the Innkeeper and in 1835 it lists Margaret Turner, it is not known if she was the wife of Philip. No further mention of the White Lion is made but we understand that it ceased to function in the 1830's. Studies of later census' reveal nothing.

The White Lion Inn c.1825

We do know, however, that the White Lion Inn became White Lion Farm. The right hand side of the building was demolished to make way for the widening of the A158, Lincoln Road. The left hand side is now R. Wisby Butcher's and White Lion Cottage, at the rear of the shop, is on the Lincoln Road.

Red Lion

The Red Lion is another establishment that we know very little about and also poses a bit of a mystery. It lays on the East side of Market Place roughly in the area of where the public toilets and the CB shop are now. Behind this is Red Lion Cottage, which was formerly the living quarters of the Landlords of the Public House. The cottage is now a private residence and the current owner has sympathetically outlined, in engineering bricks on the cottage wall, the position of access from the original Public House to the Landlord's quarters.

It was customary for the ostlers and horses of the carriages to stay overnight at the Red Lion while the passengers stayed at the Turnor Arms.   The selling of corn and cattle was also carried out here.

It first appears in the Directories in 1828, listing Charles Hurst as the Innkeeper and in 1841 we find that Elizabeth Hurst has taken over. In the 1856 Directory George Pickwell is now the Proprietor and here the mystery begins. George is listed as Innkeeper and Farmer of 20 acres, in both the 1861 and 1871 census' and again in the directory of 1872. The census of 1871 states that George is 51 years of age, is married and has three children: George who is 19 and an Agricultural Labourer; Emily at 19 is Housemaid and Susannah who is just 15 and is a Barmaid.

The Red Lion c1875

The mystery is that in the 1881 census the whole family as well as the Red Lion have disappeared from Wragby! All except for young George who is now lodging with Mary Brothwell and her family in Bardney Road. From further research it would appear that Emily married Matthias Sutton in 1871 and moved to Barnetby-le-Wold. Susannah appears to have married George Rowson in 1879, and moved to West Torrington. From the records it is possible that the elder George died in 1877 and Mary in 1879, but what happened to the Red Lion? The Inn is still missing even though we had understood that the Red Lion did not cease trading until 1895.

Adam & Eve

In appearance the Adam & Eve, on the junction of the Horncastle and Louth Roads, looks to be the oldest Inn but it is not directly mentioned in the Directories until 1828. The proprietor of that time was Benjamin Harrison and he, or perhaps his father, is mentioned in 1792 as a Farmer and Victualler, so perhaps the Adam & Eve was in business then but was not a principal Inn.

In 1872, a Lodge of Foresters was held here, having 180 members and a capital of £800. They are mentioned again in 1891 as having a Court of Foresters but now with 207 members and a capital of £1600. Unfortunately they are not mentioned again but we understand that they used to meet throughout the county.

The Adam & Eve in the 1930s
(Thanks to Barry Ward)

The list of Proprietors is shown below, again from the Directories and relevant Census'.

1826	Benjamin Harrison
1835 and 1841	Edward Clark
1856 and 1861	Mary and Joseph Clark (Farmer and Victualler)
1871 and 1872	Mrs. E. Clark (Victualler and Farmer)
1881. 1891 and 1905	George Phillipson (Victualler and Farmer)
	Note: On the census it is George with no Charles in the household but in the Directories 1889 Charles is listed as Innkeeper)
1909	Joseph Phillipson (in 1913 Joseph had taken over the Turnor Arms)
1937	Alfred Arthur Child
1941 onwards	Mr. & Mrs. Wattam

One can only assume that the Adam & Eve was closed for a time because no mention of it was made in the 1913 or 1919 Directories. One interesting point - in 1940 the license fee for the Adam & Eve cost £80 a year and lasted for three years.

Others

The Ivy Club, was a private dwelling, which was opened as a Working Men's Club in 1927 and we believe is still listed as a private club.

The Corn Dolly is a relatively new enterprise and is a licensed restaurant. Both are situated on the West side of the Market Place.

The following picture depicts both premises after ten inches of snow fell on Good Friday, 1975. Tom Clowes, Landlord of the Ivy Club, is seen clearing snow from the front of the club. Although he was the Landlord, Tom apparently never served beer, but preferred to sit in the back room. The other gentleman is Ted Alcock entering the Corn Dolly heading for his favourite table. The snow eventually cleared at around 3 o'clock that afternoon.

Good Friday 1975 - Market Place

❖ ❖

Wedding by Erica Clark Gosling - 9th October 1964
*My sister Christine was bridesmaid at a very pretty wedding a week last Saturday. We went down to the
Adam and Eve chalet to see the bride and bridesmaids come*

The Black and White Concert Party as they appeared in 'Contrasts'

Front Row: Charles Stromberg, Binkie Bartholomew, Peggy Potter, Edward Wattam, Molly Bartholomew, Trot Weightman, Edith Wilkinson, Leslie Thorne
Back Row: Albert Elwick, Dorothy Hayward, John Hayward, Pat Seely, Betty Hayward, Edmund Bartholomew, Isobel Paul, Alice Dove, Margaret Seely, Stan Hayward

Forerunners of the present Wragby Players
Including: John Robinson, Edward Wattam, Reg Skipworth, Alice Dove and Les Thorne

ENTERTAINMENT

The Wragby Minstrels

The Wragby Minstrels were formed in 1929 and from then until 1932 entertained Wragby and District with many concerts. True to minstrel style they performed with blacked faces and included in their repertoire were songs like *'Swannee River'*, *'Camptown Races'*, *'Poor Old Joe'* among others.

The concerts were apparently one of the earliest efforts to raise funds for a proposed 'Town Hall' and it is thought that they raised the princely sum of £40, a substantial amount during a time of great depression.

WRAGBY NIGGER MINSTREL TROUPE 1929-30

The Wragby Minstrels

L-R: Mr. A.W. Mumby (Conductor and Violin) Charlie Whitehead, Sydney Rowson, Joe Dixon, Reggie Skipworth, William Brothwell, Walter Rutland, Joseph Paul (interlocuter), Jack Anderson, Godfrey Holmes, Fred Thorne, Pat Picksley, Charlie Wilson, Sid Bradshaw (tambourine), Mrs. J. Paul (Piano)
Front: Dick Paul, Norman Louth and Harry Thorne. **Inset:** Walter Broxholme, as Bones (1929).

The Wragby Players

It is difficult to say when the first Wragby Players got started or who they were. It would appear that the people of Wragby have always had the ability to entertain themselves and arrange concerts and the like for the area.

We have already mentioned the Minstrels but in 1946 another group of entertainers was making its name as The Black and White Concert Party. In December of that year they put on a Revue called *'Contrasts'* in aid of the local football club funds, the proceeds of which amounted to over £18.   The Revue was held in the Chalet and comprised original sketches, songs and a quiz. The concert was performed in the afternoon for the older people, after which they enjoyed a splendid tea.   The evening performance culminated with a dance.

One particular concert contained *'Lily Marlene'*, *'Songs of the Islands'* complete with grass skirts, *'Down in the Valley'*, *'Bless You'*, *'Let him Go, Let him Tarry'* and *'Down on the Farm'*.

The present day Wragby Players originally got together on 6th February 1974 and decided to form an amateur dramatic society. The committee members appointed were Messrs. R. Crimble, T. Neale, E. Green and E. McGrath, Mrs. Miller and Miss B. Scott.

Their first production was *'Summer Salad'* a revue providing family entertainment, produced by Tony Neale, and was performed on 7th - 8th May 1974. Admission prices were 30p per adult and 15p per child. That same year, on 15th - 16th November, they staged two one act plays *'Woman Alive'* by John Tulley and *'Wife Required'* by Falkland L. Cary and Philip Kink. Refreshments were served between the plays which were produced by Mrs. M. Harper from Belchford.

Having perhaps peaked in the time of the 'musicals' Wragby Players are still going strong today through the determination of a dedicated group of enthusiastic members. Some productions do not get the support they need although the 'Evenings of Entertainment' and the children's 'Pantomimes' are usually very well attended.

The Chalet

In today's terms we wouldn't think very much of a wood lined, corrugated iron shed, but in the mid 1930's one became the hub of all social activity in Wragby.

The origin of the Chalet is not fully known, but it was used as a temporary hospital for servicemen during WWI and was purchased from Monks Abbey School, Lincoln in about 1934/35. It was dismantled, transported to Wragby and re-erected in the Adam & Eve car park by Arthur Rutland and his team of workmen, which included Tom Shepherd and George Dales.

The Chalet

Once sited the Chalet served refreshments to the passengers of the numerous coaches, which were en route to and from the coast on a daily basis. This 'day-tripper' trade was a roaring success and it was not unusual for up to 70 coaches to be parked in the Market Place or Adam & Eve car parks. This was not so unusual as it was the heyday of the 'Charabanc'. Few people had their own transport and petrol was not easy to obtain. The coaches came from all round the area, especially the East Midlands, Yorkshire and Derbyshire, for a day at Skegness. On the return journey too, they would stop and indulge in fish and chips and a beer after enjoying themselves at the seaside.

Prior to the arrival of the Chalet, local dances used to be held in what is now the Youth Cluband whist drives were held in the Old Grammar School. With the arrival of the Chalet all social activities were centred there. In fact it became the hub of all social life in the village, holding wedding receptions, film shows, revues and auction sales as well as the dances – when the service personnel nicknamed it the 'sweatbox'. The building had its own stage and had pretty curtains at the windows, which made it an ideal entertainment centre. Some of the people who ran the Youth Club at the Chalet during that period were Colin Skipworth, Rex Keal, Judy Stephenson, Jean Clark (now Turner) and Joyce Clark.

Unfortunately wars bring change and at the outbreak of WWII the 'day-tripper' trade virtually dried up with petrol rationing and the closure of beaches. The Chalet was taken over by the Army and about 100 men were able to sleep there while waiting for their overseas postings. Not all was gloom however, central heating was installed, ENSA provided dances and entertainments and some of the servicemen swelled the numbers in the church choir. The forces also boosted the locals' social life, as at that time Wragby's population was only about 500.

After the war, although the Chalet still held social events the 'day-trip' coach trade never really resumed as people couldn't afford such luxury with rationing. When the Town Hall was built in 1954 the Chalet became virtually redundant as the social focal point. The Adam & Eve still used the Chalet up to the mid 1970's and it was then taken over by a local businessman to act as a warehouse.

Old age, natural deterioration and damage caused by violent storms in 1990 proved the death knell for the Chalet and it was finally dismantled and removed. Although the Chalet is no longer there, it lives on in the minds of many people and is remembered with fondness and nostalgia.

Darby & Joan

The *Dictionary of National Biography(DNB)* states that the name Darby & Joan originated when a Henry Woodfall was apprenticed to John Darby, a printer who lived in Bartholomew Close in the City of London (Woodfall was later a well-known person in London, he became the printer of the *Public Advertiser* in Paternoster Row and was appointed as master of the *Stationers' Company* in 1766). John Darby died in 1730 and the *DNB* says Woodfall wrote a ballad/poem, published in *The Gentleman's Magazine* in 1735, to commemorate his late employer John and his wife Joan. Their names became synonymous with marital affection.

Members of Wragby Darby and Joan Club at an Annual Party
The Photograph is as it appeared in The Standard but no date given

It has not been possible to pin-point just when the Wragby Club, for retired residents, was formed. However, Flo Shepherd can remember attending in the Reading Room sometime after the end of the Second World War. When the Town Hall was built, in 1954, they used to meet there on a Thursday afternoon and the members played cards, dominoes and other games and finishing with tea.

For many years it was led by, Mrs Edgar Thorne, who was older than many of the members. Later Mrs. Flo Bones took over but numbers began to decline and other leaders were not forthcoming. It is not known precisely when it ended but the final meeting was of a meal at the Adam and Eve.

Garden Fete by K. Martin - 10th July 1964
There was a Fete at Wragby last Saturday and there was also one at Wickenby. At Wickenby they got about £160. My daddy won a pig at Wickenby on the skittles.

TRANSPORT AND ESSENTIAL SERVICES

Road

As has been mentioned earlier, although no hard evidence exists regarding a settlement at Wragby in Roman times, it is highly likely that a road linked the established settlements of Horncastle and Lincoln.

When Turnpike Roads introduced during the 18th century, Wragby was on the Turnpike from Lincoln to Horncastle, Louth and the coast. In 1791, the post arrived from London on a Sunday and two carriers from London passed through once a week. Coaches from Hull to Boston passed through Wragby every day at five o'clock and the 'Pelham' came through at half past nine every morning on its way to Hull, via Market Rasen, Caistor, Limber and New Ferry. The 'Protector' left Louth daily, via Wragby, for Lincoln and also in the reverse direction. Regular mail gigs left daily for Horncastle and Lincoln. The Turnor Arms and the White Lion were used as posting houses. For anyone who did not have their own transport, carriers also left every week from the Turnor Arms to attend the markets at Horncastle, Hull and Lincoln.

Notations from 1792 reveal that the post from London now arrived on Sunday, Wednesday and Friday evenings; the two carriers also still came through.

In 1826 the stagecoach 'Champion' left Wragby daily for Lincoln at 11 o'clock in the mornings, and to Horncastle and Louth at 4 o'clock in the afternoons.

Toll Booth

Wragby's Toll Booth was situated on the Horncastle Road, next to Turner Square and opposite the Adam & Eve. As one of the first in the Country, it was of major importance. Some time after its closure in the late 1800's it was used as a shop.

TOLL GATE CHARGES GEO.III 1806

For every Horse and Beast of draught, drawing any coach/vehicle the sum of THREE PENCE.

For every Horse or Beast of draught, drawing any wagon wain cart or other carriage having the Sole or Bottom of the Fellies of the wheels thereof the breadth of Six Inches THREEPENCE As above-- but if the Sole or Bottom of the Fellies thereof have a less breadth than Six Inches - the sum of FOURPENCE HALFPENNY.

For every Home Mare Gelding Mule or Ass or other beast of burden, not drawing-- the sum of ONE PENNY and ONE HALFPENNY.

For every drove of Oxen, Cows or neat Cattle, the sum of TEN PENCE per score and so in proportion for any greater or less number.

For every Drove of Calves, Hogs, Sheep or Lambs the sum of FIVE PENCE per score, and so on in proportion or any greater or lesser number.

Roadmen

Joseph Bratley and a boy named Markham, who used to be a post boy, worked on the upkeep of the roads. At the beginning they only worked certain months of the year and filled in time by harvesting and other agricultural work. Then they had to dig the gravel from the pits, then break it up before it was fit to place on the roads. Joseph said he was "mighty pleased" when the gravel eventually came already broken up. The roads in some places were in a very bad condition, the ruts being deep and uneven. The roadmen had some unpleasant remarks thrown at them by the drivers of vehicles. However, the roads in the Wragby area were very good compared to other districts. When they were all taken over by the council, other roads required so much more doing to them than the Wragby roads. Wragby residents thought it hardly fair for them to share in the cost.

Railway

A line was eventually arranged from Bardney to Louth, to run through Wragby and men came down to measure the ground. This caused a great deal of local interest, and perhaps a little grumbling. A Mr. Dawson, of Withcall, objected greatly to the people coming to measure across his lands, and absolutely refused to allow them to proceed. The surveyors were not to be denied and Mr. Bratley formed a party of two caravans, at midnight one Sunday, when Dawson was asleep. The surveyors went across the objector's land and the required measurements were obtained. When he knew he had been outwitted Mr. Dawson's face must have been a picture. He vowed he would have thrown the whole lot of them in the horse pond, if he had caught them. Bratley said, *"I reckon he would have had a job, for there was a rare lot of us".* The line was commenced, requiring much carting away of soil and Mr. Dawson enjoyed many a ride in the carts taking the soil to Donnington on Bain.

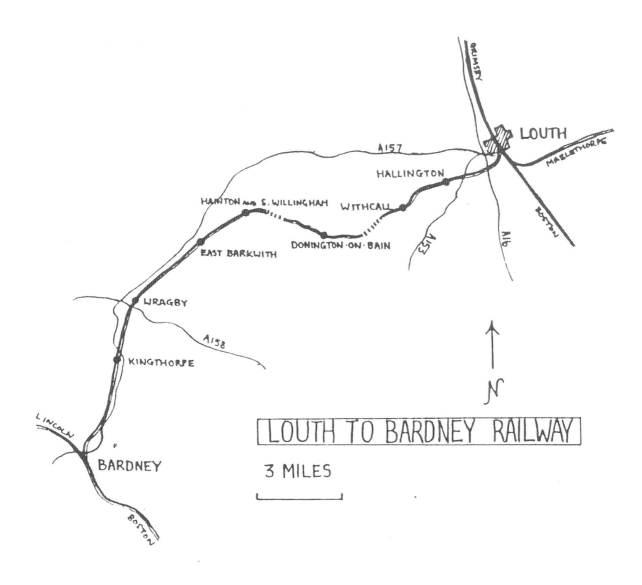

The line was opened on 1st December 1876, with construction costs amounting to £380,000, partly due to having to tunnel at Willingham and Withcall. The original railway company, called the Louth-Lincoln Company, was bought in 1872 by the Great Northern Railway, reputedly for £200,000.

Wragby Station 1907

As with most railways, passenger services ceased in 1951 and the cessation of goods trains marked the final closure in 1960.

'Born 1876 - Died 1951 In Memoriam, RIP' - this was the inscription on the large wreath which decorated the smoke-box door of the last passenger train to stop at Wragby on its way to Louth from Bardney. Stationmaster, Mr. E.W. Savoury, had placed it there earlier in the day when the train made its last journey to Bardney.

C12 4-4-2 6379 The last Passenger Train leaves Wragby Station

To mark the historic event, a small crowd of spectators had braved the heavy rain and gathered in the dimly lit station. Fireworks and cheers sent the train on its way as it left the station - more in keeping with an opening not a closing. Several railway enthusiasts were among those who had bought the last tickets.

Courtesy of Lincolnshire Chronicle 1951

The last passengers to board the train, at Wragby, were Mrs. Fanny Richardson and Margaret Homes, both of Willingham. An enthusiast bought the last ticket to be issued at the station, to East Barkwith.

The Last Goods Train - 1960
Photo: Dick Bones

It had been agreed, to keep the track open for goods traffic and would come under the control of Donnington-on-Bain, who used the line extensively during the war for carrying bombs for the RAF. stationed there.

The final journey by a goods train was in 1960 when the Bardney - Louth line closed completely; the track was lifted in 1961.

However, that is not the end of the line. There were numerous stories about a phantom train and, in 1969, the story was tested by two intrepid sceptics. They drove to Hallington station where the station house was now occupied by the local shepherd. Having been refused permission to park in the yard they drove further down the lane facing the station and parked there, with just a field of sheep to keep them company. On a fine summer evening the silence was broken about 11:45 p.m. by the faint sound of what seemed to be a steam train approaching and working hard to climb the hill. As the sound grew it was possible to hear the occasional clunk of the wagon couplings and the distinctive clank of the rods. The sound got louder and louder coming in waves as if driven by the wind, but the spell was broken by the barking of dogs. They then noticed that the sheep had stampeded to the far side of the field. The sound continued very faintly now, as if moving to Withcall; the dogs quieted and the sheep settled and once more there was the silence of the night.

It is still possible to walk the course of the line in some places. The residue of the Great Northern Railway can still be seen today; the old Station House, now privately owned, is just next door to the new housing development which occupies the old petrol station site, and the old platform can easily be seen from the road.

Signal Box - Wragby 1912

Mail Services

1821-2000

The first postmaster noted in the records was William Stephenson, who was also a watch and clockmaker. In 1821, the posting house was the Nag's Head Inn, now the Turnor Arms. Mail used to arrive from Lincoln, Horncastle and Market Rasen in the evening of each day and from London, weekly on Sundays.

From 1826 to 1857, William Pickering was postmaster, who also had a drapers shop in the Market Place. Throughout the years the mail service changed considerably, even though it still arrived and was despatched by horse driven coaches. Mail to London and the South was despatched in the morning and to Horncastle and Market Rasen in the evening on a daily basis. Incoming mail arrived in the morning. This changed again in 1842, when letters to London left at 12:30 pm and those for the North at 8:00 pm.

By 1856, the rail system was being used for mail and letters were being despatched at 7:00 am. Langworth Station was in use in 1848 and the post cart went every day from Wragby. There were four Post Messengers, listed in the census of 1861 living in Wragby.

After the death of William Pickering, in 1857, his widow, Anne Elizabeth, carried out the duties of the Post Office and still kept the drapers shop. Although not listed as a postmistress in the 1861 census, Ann Elizabeth Pickering is mentioned in the Directory for 1865 as the receiver of letters. Her daughter, Emily Anne, aged 13, worked as a domestic servant for her Uncle, a surgeon called John D. Wrangham.

The census of 1871 shows that Anne Elizabeth Pickering was the postmistress with her daughter, Emily Anne as her assistant. They now lived in Victoria Street, near the Police Station, and they had a domestic helper, Rebecca Knoll, aged 19. In addition to the mail, the Post Office acted as a bank to 350 depositors and a Telegraph Service was in use.

In 1891, Emily Anne took over the office from her mother, her assistant was, Jane Hunt and Hepzibah A. Dean was their domestic servant. Letters arrived at 7:17 am and 6:25 pm and were despatched at 10:25

am and 6:15 pm, for Lincoln. Emily Anne retired as postmistress in 1906. In total the Pickering family handled Wragby's post for 80 years.

William Arthur Spofforth took over as postmaster after Emily Anne retired. He was also a grocer in the Market Place, with premises where the current Post Office is situated, and a Parish Councillor. Mail arrived slightly earlier at 7:00 am and 6:25 pm from London and the South and was despatched at 10:15 am and 6:25 pm.

When Mr. Spofforth retired in 1913, the position of postmaster was taken by George Thomas Sutton, who also took over the shop. Mr. Sutton eventually purchased the premises from the Panton Estate for £250. He ran the business with his wife, who had worked at the Post Office before her marriage. In 1922 a telegram service was introduced. Mrs. Sutton looked after the postal side and switchboard, which in the 1930's was the old peg style connection, while Mr. Sutton looked after the drapers and tailors shop.

George Sutton retired, after 33 years service as postmaster, handing over to his son, Geoff, in 1946. Mr. Geoff Sutton died in 1963, and with no family to carry on the business is was sold to Mr. and Mrs. Brian Melton in 1984. Mr. Alan Woodward took over and it was sold to Mr. Glenn Marflitt in 1994. The Post Office has been situated on the same site for 100 years and only four families have run the business during the last century.

Before the post code system was introduced, mail for the district arrived at Lincoln to be sorted and sent to Wragby to be further sorted by Postmen/women at Wragby Post Office. Since then all Lincoln area mail arrives at Doncaster and is then sent to the Lincoln Office for further sorting. The mail for the Wragby area is sent to Market Rasen for local sorting.

Postal Workers outside the Post Office at the closure of the Sorting Office

**From Left to Right:
Jim Sutherland, Kathy Lowe,
Thelma Humberston, Benny Hinchliffe,
Alan Woodward PM, Marlene Scurr and
Kath Cannon**

Communications

The first telegraph system was operated from the post office in, Victoria Street, next to the Police Station, by the post mistress, Mrs. Anne Elizabeth Pickering. It would be between 1871-1881 and it probably consisted of a two wire overhead line to the Lincoln telegraph office, with a local instrument, to send in Morse code.

In 1922 a telegram service was introduced from the Post Office, which was now at the present site in the Market Place. Between 1922 and 1926 a small switchboard was installed and subscribers were connected to it. In 1937, there were less than 100 subscribers, with numbers still in single and double figures.

Wragby was due to go automatic in 1938 but as war broke out in 1939 the system was delayed. The exchange in Silver Street was built around 1949-50. Originally it would have accommodated 300 to 400 lines and junctions. Probably U.A.X (unit auto exchange no.13) later this was extended to accommodate more (u.a.xl3x).

The next move was to Lincoln Road in the 1970's. The exchange may have been electronic as they were installed at that time. By 1979 (S.T.D) subscribers trunk dialling was completed which meant all exchanges were automatic.

Today the exchange in Lincoln Road is of the modern computer controlled type and many of the outlying exchanges in the area have disappeared. The system has been developed over the last 20 years, due to advanced technology, and the service and facilities offered cannot be compared to the systems of forty years ago.

Following an initiative by the Wragby Heritage Group, the required minimum of 300 signatures, from genuinely interested parties, were obtained for the availability of Broadband. This facility was made available to Wragby in 2004.

Post Office and Turnor Arms 1930

Water Supply

1850 to 1998

Before 1850 the inhabitants of Wragby depended on the wells that were scattered about the town, of which there were 26 marked on the map of 1891. These were sunk into the sandstone lying below the surface of the soil. Rainwater would soak through and saturate the sandstone that was underlaid by the Kimmerage Clay which is impervious, holding the water shelf at a fluctuating level according to the amount of rain falling. This was quite satisfactory except that wells could fail in very dry weather and sometimes the water would be contaminated and cause illness to the consumers. (See extracts of Parish Council Minutes).

In the 1860's a water works provided water for domestic use from the beck, close to Wragby. The water works, provided by the owner of Panton Estate, Christopher Turnor, consisted of building a dam and weir upstream of the Langton Bridge, and laying a pipeline from this reservoir to a tank, set up on top of the Market House, together with a hydraulic ram situated 80 yards on the Wragby side of the bridge for lifting. The water could then run by gravity from the tank to the taps.

In 1912 a fresh, clean water supply was obtained from a spring on the Panton Estate. A pipe was laid to bring this water down to a point below the ram and so the many difficulties of the pollution of the beck, by sheep washing and consequent contamination of the water supply was overcome. This resulted in better health for the inhabitants.

Christopher Turnor did not charge the Parish Council for this work, or for the use of the water when it previously came from the beck, but now he did make a charge.

Extract from Parish Council Minutes 1913:

Water Rates

The agent explained that Mr. Turnor was charging the Parish with interest on £1000 at 5% p.a. £50 plus £10 p.a. for upkeep making a total of £60 (Farmers would have the surplus water for stock, free.)

This was the position up to 1917 when the estate was sold.

Extract from Parish Council Minutes May 23rd 1917:

Mr. Hutchinson the agent to C. E. Turnor Esq. met the Parish Council at this meeting and offered, on behalf of the owner, to give to the Parish of Wragby the whole system of water supply, namely :

> The right to draw the water from Panton.
> The pipes and wayleaves through his property and to secure the wayleaves for the future.
> The mains and pipes he now owns.
> The storage tank in the Market Place and all the apparatus belonging to the present supply.

The Parish Council having no legal standing to accept this offer, instructed the clerk to bring the matter before the Rural district Council.

Approximately a year later the Rural District Council had taken over the supply. This was the position up to 1936 when a new water source was obtained near Benniworth which would run by gravity to Wragby. There was no need for the hydraulic ram or the tank in the system.

Sewage Treatment Works

Originally established in the late 1960's by Horncastle Rural District Council, the Wragby Sewage Treatment Works serves the villages of Wragby and East and West Barkwith. It treats the sewage to a high standard and discharges final effluent to a small stream which flows alongside the works and eventually joins the River Witham.

The works was built in two stages. The old works consisted of a small primary tank, followed by two small filters, which are no longer used, and a small humus tank. The works was extended, at a later date, by the addition of a large radial primary tank, a new inlet works, two large new filters, a new radial humus tank and an upward flow pebble clarifier.

Flows enter the inlet works and pass through a macerator which chops up large material. The flow is then split between the two primary tanks, prior to passing through the two large filters. The flow then receives secondary settlement in the two humus tanks.

Due to the tight consent standard of 20mg/.1 Biochemical Oxygen Demand and 20mg/.1 Suspended Solids, the flows receive tertiary treatment in the pebble clarifier prior to discharge to the stream.

Sludge from the primary tanks is stored in two sludge holding tanks before being removed by tanker for spreading onto agricultural land, where its soil conditioning properties are much appreciated.

WRAGBY SEWAGE TREATMENT WORKS

Police

By the 1850's, crime in Wragby was such that it was thought necessary to have a local court. The Courthouse was built in 1855 to the standard pattern adopted in Lindsey and included a Police Station and cells. Once built, the Court served as the headquarters for the Wragby petty session's division and a magistrate's court was held there on the first Thursday of the month. Meetings of the Assessors of Property Taxes were also held there.

Wragby Police House and Court

During the early 20th century, Wragby had easily the most aristocratic bench of magistrates in the county. The Chairman of the Bench was the first Lord Heneage, who regularly presided over the monthly courts until the 1914-18 war. Sometimes a groom drove him from Hainton Hall, and sometimes he drove himself in a little dogcart. For many years the Vice-chairman was Preston Rawnsley, one of the best hunting squires Lincolnshire has ever known. Edmund Turnor MP, of Panton Hall, was another well-known magistrate. A number of clergymen too sat on the Bench. One such was Canon W. Moore, vicar of Wragby, about whom the story is told that on one occasion he sentenced a poacher to *six* months in prison. Whereupon the poacher told him he couldn't do that, as the maximum was three months. After consulting with his clerk, the Canon, without acknowledging the interruption, calmly repeated his sentencing statement but with three months substituted instead of the erroneous six months.

The minute books show that over 50 years ago, begging was quite a problem in Wragby. Tramps on their way from Lincoln to either Horncastle or Louth had made it a regular stop. Calling at houses begging for money or bread. Such cases usually brought seven days imprisonment but sometimes it was 21 days. These cases were usually brought before the clergy magistrates, who regularly sentenced offenders to seven days in jail. One typical case from the 1920's minute book shows how justice was meted out at the beginning of the century.

One Charles Murray, of no fixed abode, was charged with begging and pleaded not guilty. Apparently Murray had called at the house of a Mr. Briggs and asked for a drink, Mr. Briggs showed him the pump. Murray then asked for some food. Mr. Briggs complained to the police and the constable set off after Murray. The minute book states that the constable told Murray "You have been begging in a public place". Whereupon Murray replied, "No, I have not". Murray was searched by the constable and was found to have in his possession one shilling and ten pence in money, a corn cure and two pawn tickets. He was taken to the Wragby lockup and next day sentenced to seven days in prison.

In 1965, a move towards centralisation linked the Lindsey and Wragby courts to Lincoln but did not otherwise affect the court. However, by 1971 the Lindsey Magistrate Courts Committee had decided to phase out Wragby and later that year the court was closed, although the building continued in use as a police station for some time afterwards.

On 28th February 1990, a new Police station was opened in Silver Street.   The new office, built at a cost of £64,000 consists of a reception area, office with store, lobby and toilet facilities and a garage.

1906

Excerpt from *The Mail*, Saturday February 3rd 1906

A Prosaic Courtship at Wragby

So it was described at Suffolk Assizes at Ipswich when, before Mr. Justice Lawrence, an action was heard in which Miss Ethel Wheelhouse, of Ipswich, sued Robert William Clark, a veterinary surgeon, a widower, of Beech House, Wragby, for damages for breach of promise of marriage.

Apparently in response to a reply to an advertisement for a lady housekeeper Miss Wheelhouse received a communication from Mr. Clark in which he described himself as a widower, a veterinary surgeon, 37 years of age with no family. He kept only one servant who could cook and do all the work. He said he had quite as good a position socially as the local medical man and had two brothers in the medical profession. As a matter of fact he was in a good position, kept several horses, hunted, shot, raced, motored and was invited to most of the local social gatherings including an 'At Home' given by a lady of title.

Miss Wheelhouse commenced her duties on April 16th and as the parties got to know each other better she said that he seemed to make overtures of a more affectionate nature. On one day whilst boating, she said that he said he would like to marry her and would buy her a ring when they got back ashore. However he could not buy a ring as he only had £4 in his pocket and didn't want to pay by cheque as then all would know how much he had paid for it, and that she should keep the engagement quiet for now.

When she went back to Ipswich for a short stay he wrote to her signing the letter yours faithfully, Bob and later My dear Ethel and signed Yours faithfully, Bob. However, according to Miss Wheelhouse he was trying to get out of the arrangement and wrote a letter designed to break off the engagement. As she was home at that time he suggested that she did not come back until after camp (he was in the Yeomanry).

He also apparently gave false replies as to his income stating that it was £188 per year, but after considerable trouble the plaintiff's lawyer found that in 1905 his income was £605.

Mr. Clark's answer to this action was that on May 31st 1905 the contract to marry was, by mutual consent, rescinded. However, there was no letter to back this up. After giving evidence and amid much hilarity in court over her expectations and as money was not obtained by Mr. Clark despite Miss Wheelhouse's offer to loan him some money, the Judge found in favour of Miss Wheelhouse and awarded her £5 in damages.

Fire Brigade

The earliest documentation we have of the Wragby Fire Brigade is a copy of the "Rules" drawn up on 3rd December 1868, which show that a crew of six firemen was envisaged. From its earliest days the Fire Station was in the Buttermarket, now Gothic House take-away, and if viewed from the rear of the building the water tank can still be seen.

In 1875 when Mr. Wedd Henry Dove was Captain the fire appliance would have been a horse drawn, pumping vehicle. It wasn't until 1926, when Len Johnson, Brigade Captain, converted an old bean lorry to a fire engine, that we had a mechanical pump, taken from an old horse drawn tender, on the back instead of the separate towing one. The converted lorry was operational until 1938.

The old Bean Lorry Fire Engine

There were no water tenders in those days, a local pond or beck was the only supply for water to dampen the fires. Mains water was brought to Wragby in 1934 but most houses had an iron pump or a well in the garden.

When Len joined the Fire Service in 1921, little did he realise he would be starting a dynasty of Johnson firefighters. His son, Arthur followed him in 1936 and became Section Leader in 1942 serving a total of 37 years. Ken Johnson, Arthur's son, became Sub Officer in 1970 and retired in 1995 after 38 years service. His son, John, was fortunate in replacing his father as Sub Officer at Wragby and Ken's other son, Neil is now Watch Manager.

It is also worth mentioning that all Wragby fire personnel are retained firefighters, and that when Arthur Johnson joined in 1936 he was on a £5 per year retainer.

During the 1939-45 war, 26 men were on call to extinguish fires, using a six seater Humber car and an American Terraplane V8 towing vehicle. These vehicles were painted grey and it was only after the war that they were repainted red, which has continued to the present day. In 1944 the Wragby Fire Brigade became part of the National Fire Service and had 15 staff.

In the 1950's a red Ford V8 van was used, pulling a Harland pump behind. The van was kept in the Market Place garage of the old buttermarket with the pump located at J.B. Johnson's garage in Bardney Road.

National Fire Service Wragby 1944

Back Row L-R: E. Tuplin, T. Keal, G. Cannon, P. Scaife
Middle L-R: Fred Johnson, C. Clark, M. Tuplin, E. Meanwell, F. Hobson
Front L-R: A. Johnson, A. Wilkinson, S. Scaife, H. Dixon, G. Kitchen, A. Rutland

Mrs. Phyllis Johnson used to activate the siren to call the firemen, some running to start the engine and others to get the pump ready. When up and running, the fire engine carried a crew of 12 men, ten riding in the back with the driver and bell ringer in front.

The new fire station was built in 1954, where it stands today, and in the 1960's it was equipped with a Bedford fire tender with a water tank pump as standard. The community fire station, as it is now known, is supplied with the most modern fire fighting appliances available and also attends incidents as First Responders.

Wragby Fire Service 2007
Kathy Dunn, Crew Manager and Neil Johnson, Watch Manager

RULES

REGULATION OF THE FIRE BRIGADE AT WRAGBY.

I.   THAT the Engineer have charge of the Fire Engine and be responsible for the safety thereof, and of all the buckets, implements, and stores provided; and be also responsible for the efficiency of the Engine and its being in readiness for service at the shortest notice.

II.   That the Firemen receive directions only from the Captain, or in the absence of the Captain the Engineer and promptly and strictly obey orders,

III   That each Fireman be numbered.

IV.   That on information of a fire reaching any officer of the brigade, he do immediately—

  1. Cause the fire bell to be rung.
  2. Procure a key of and open the Engine-house.
  3. Send Messengers to the Inn for horses to be got ready (should the Engine be   required to leave the Town.)
  4. Send Messengers to the Engineer and other Members of the brigade.

   No fireman to leave the Engine-house unless directed by the Engineer or Captain.

V.   That it shall be the duty of the firemen on their arrival at the Engine-house after an alarm of fire, to attend to the following instructions: —

FIREMAN. No. 1. To provide the proper quantity of buckets and place them on the Engine, and be responsible for the return of the quantity taken out of the Engine house: (this duty may be readily performed by putting 10 buckets on each string).

No, 2.   To see that the suction, delivery, and service pipes are in their proper places in the Engine, and secured in a proper manner, and be responsible for their safety and return.

No. 3   To see that all tools, forks, hooks, &c., are properly secured in their proper places on the Engine, and be responsible for their safe return.

No. 4   To see that the lamps are supplied with candles, —that the lynch pins and fastenings of the Engine are safe, and to prevent persons from getting upon the Engine.

No. 5 and 6. To fasten in the pole or hand-rail of the Engine, keep the Engine-house clear, and when the Engine is drawn out assist No. 1 in securing- the bucket rails. &c.

The Engineer to see that the pipe key and tools kept in his box are in their places, both in going out and returning with the Engine.

VI.   That no person but a member of the fire brigade or his deputy, be allowed to ride upon the Engine

VII   *That on arrival at a fire,* the Captain or Engineer shall point out the proper place for the Engine to be stationed, and then make arrangements for procuring a proper supply of water, and hands to work the Engine.

The Engineer shall immediately get the Engine into gear, and himself take charge of the service pipe and generally take charge of the Engine and direct the firemen, &c, until the fire is extinguished.

Unless otherwise directed by the Captain

FIREMEN Nos. 1 and 5, To take off the buckets and pass them to the water edge (returning the strings to the box), and then attend to the working of the Engine.

Nos. 2 and 6, To take out and affix the proper pipes to the Engine, returning the key to the box, and No 2 to see that the pipes are kept clear.

Nos. 3 and 4, To take the water tub to the water edge if necessary, and sink it (and returning to the Engine take off any of the tools that may be required.)

VI11   When the fire is extinguished, each officer will collect and affix to the Engine the articles for which he is responsible, and report any damaged or missing articles to the Engineer.

NB   The above Regulations to be observed as much as possible when the Engines are drawn out for *trial*, that the men may become accustomed to their several duties.

By order of the Committee,

WILLIAM SEAGRAVE,

WRAGBY DEC. 3RD 1868   HON. SECRETARY AND TREASURER

HORNCASTLE RURAL EMERGENCY TEAMS.

Local Organiser: Mrs. S. Wood, Garth House, Baumber.
                                         Tel: Baumber 210.

WRAGBY.

Leader: Mrs. R. Bones, "Kinver", Silver Street, Wragby.
                                         Tel: Wragby 858471.

Deputy: Mrs. R. Shuttleworth, The Manor, Langton-by-Wragby.
                                         Tel: Wragby 858220.

Teams: "A"   Mrs. R. Bones.   Tel: Wragby 858471.

                 Mrs. Martin   "   858236.

           *   Mrs. Sutherland   "   858492.

                 Miss Green   "   858337.

         , *   Mrs. Bourn   "   858352.

          "B"   Mrs. Shuttleworth   "   858220.

                 Mrs. Grantham   "   858425.

                 Mrs. Miller   "   858543.

Callout   Leader rings deputy.
procedure   Leader rings list "A"
                 Deputy rings list "B"
                 Deputy reports to Leader
                 Leader reports to local organiser.

County Council Area Rest Centre:

                 Wragby Primary School   Tel: Wragby 858 477.
                 Headmaster:
                 Mr. G. Burbage   . Tel: Baumber 601.

                 Caretaker:
                 Mr. T. Shepherd   Tel: Wragby 858447.

Supplies: If bread, milk etc. have to be provided by
                 W.R.V.S., contact:

                 Mr. M. Thorneycroft, Market Place Stores, Wragby.

                                         Tel: Wragby 858252.

Uniform or W.R.V.S. overall to be worn if available.

It would be ideal if each team had an emergency box to be brought
to an emergency.

Suggested contents: Torch, radio, notebooks and pens, toiletries,
                     scissors, paper and string, wellingtons,
                     First Aid plasters and identification for car.

W.R.V.S. Urns available from:
                 (a) Mrs. B. Cook, "Viewmount", Lincoln Road,
                      Horncastle. Tel: Horncastle 2203,

                 (b) Louth W.R.V.S. Office. Tel: Louth 2332.

                 (c) Mrs. Hall, Tel: Louth 2433.

Which cars to use to be decided on availability at the time.

Team members with Aga or Calor Gas are marked *.

INDUSTRY AND COMMERCIAL

Hugh Bourn Developments (Wragby) Limited

It was a suggestion from Hugh Bourn's wife, Monica, that started the building enterprise to help supplement the income from farming. The family were living in Wragby, when a semi-detached cottage across Louth Road came up for sale; the occupier, Annie Johnson, had died. The owner of the property, Ken Howe, a manager at McKechnie Plastics who lived in the other semi, agreed a selling price of £200. This was turned into a profit of £1500, much more than could ever have been made from farming. Thus on Valentine's Day, 14th February 1972, Hugh Bourn Developments (Wragby) Limited was born.

With no previous building experience, Hugh Bourn took a course in bricklaying at Lincoln Polytechnic. The first property was built in Abbey Road, Bardney, and it was from this construction that Hugh Bourn received his NHBC status. Initially, it was decided to build three bungalows a year and in the first year this target was achieved. This was followed by eight and then 30 in the subsequent years, from which level it has risen to about 200 a year. A level maintained for the last 15 years. The company has built about half the houses in Wragby and in total about 3000 properties have been completed throughout North Lincolnshire.

In 1973/4 HBD bought out Thorne's building division. The birth of HBD saw the end of the pig farming business, although Hugh Bourn is still involved in the farming industry. For the first two years the business was run from home, then in 1975 offices were built on Louth Road; these were extended in 1979 and a lay-by was constructed for customer use.

Hugh Bourn's Office - Louth Road

HBD prided itself in maintaining a good working environment and most of its staff had been with the company for around 20 years. However, one of the problems with the construction industry is that the business has peaks and troughs and during the latter Hugh Bourn found it difficult to terminate the contracts of skilled craftsmen who had worked well as a team. Examples of long serving staff are to be seen in Dallas Stubbings, now retired, who worked at HBD as wages clerk for 24 years and David Ingamells, architect, who had been with the company for 26 years. About 300 men worked for HBD on 20 sites however the normal number was around 250.

Hugh Bourn was happy with the size of the company which specialised in building in the market towns of North Lincolnshire and had two sites under construction in Wragby. In 2006 Hugh Bourn Developments was sold to the Kier Group. However, members of the Bourn family are still members of the Board.

J.B Johnson & Sons Motor Engineers

John Baines Johnson started business in Wragby around 1879, as an engineer and blacksmith, shoeing horses and repairing all types of farm machinery. In the early 20th century, steam cultivators were replacing horses on the farms, so requiring more engineers to replace worn and broken parts, which the Johnson's were capable of undertaking. During the early 1900's a staff of 20 men and boys was employed and often fitted 300 to 400 iron hoops to cart wheels over a ten day period.

Early in the First World War the government of the day wanted a machine that would help win the war. As an expert in agricultural machinery, Sir William Tritton, Chairman of William Foster & Co. in Lincoln, was directly involved, together with Major Walter Gordon Wilson, in the development of the first 'modern' tank. J.B. Johnson assisted in the war effort by manufacturing thousands of track pins for the Matilda tanks made by William Foster & Co. During this time John's son, Len, was in the business and threshing drums, ploughs and harrows were all being repaired for local farmers.

Jack Draper's Steam Engine outside Johnson & Son

The motor vehicle was now taking over from steam trucks and Johnson's was running a successful contracting and haulage business. In 1934 Arthur, Len's son, joined the business and with the motor car becoming more plentiful for those that could afford them, they were repairing cars and selling petrol.

During the Second World War the Royal Engineers and other regiments were stationed at Wragby and their fitters and mechanics used Johnson's lathes and engineers' services to make repairs to army wagons.

Until the business finally closed in 2006, Ken and Paul, Arthur's sons, were still repairing lorries and cars at the Bardney Road premises where the business started over 120 years earlier, making it the oldest surviving trade in Wragby.

George Mawer & Co
Auctioneers, Valuers and Estate Agents

In 1880, George Mawer was a farmer and auctioneer, living in Apley. He sold land and farms and also conducted furniture sales. His son, Alwyn, joined the company in 1918 and was one of the founder members of the Auctioneers Institute. In 1919 the company became George Mawer & Son, Auctioneers and Agricultural Valuers.

They conducted live animal sales at the old Monks Road cattle market in Lincoln, where Lincoln College is now situated. Alwyn Mawer was a talented footballer and played for Wragby football club in the 1920's. He was chairman of Lincoln City F.C. for many years.

In the 1930's depression, many farmers were in serious financial difficulties. Auctioneers were kept busy selling farms and as most were selling cheaply, Mawer's were able to acquire land for themselves. In March 1931, six livestock farms were for sale within ten miles of Wragby.

After the second world war the company changed to Mawer & Cooper and in the early 1950's to George Mawer, Cooper and Burkitt. Jack Anderson was clerk/accountant to Mawer's, joining the company from school and staying 55 years at the Wragby office.

As Wragby is a market town, it held three cattle and sheep fairs a year, May 1st September 28 and 29th and the first Thursday in November. The cattle sales were held in the field to the rear of Red Lion Yard, up the passage to the east side of the Co-op shop; steel pens were erected in 1947 to supplement the timber and iron enclosures. A concrete sale ring with steps was built, where farmers could view and bid for the cattle being sold. Cattle trucks would unload the animals at the side of Dove's garage, they were then driven 100 yards, by hand, to the pens. This carried on until dwindling sales closed the animal market which was happening in many other small towns in England at the time.

Many small farms were sold and merged to make larger ones, and the bigger farmers discontinued livestock to concentrate on arable crops. Sheep and pigs were sold on Lincoln road on the old Holmes Woodyard site now a Hugh Bourn/Kier housing development. In November 1951, 420 cattle and 1,130 sheep were sold in one day which was a busy time for the farmers, haulage contractors and the auctioneers.

In the 1970's G.Mawer & Co amalgamated with Parish, Stafford Walter and Bell of Horncastle, and then later with Masons of Louth. The company was then known as Mawer, Mason and Bell. With house sales booming in the 1980's, Property Leeds UK Ltd., took over the company. It closed the Wragby office on March 30th 1990 and transferred the business to Market Rasen. This, in turn, was swallowed up by Halifax Property Services. The Mawer name has now resurfaced in Market Rasen as Perkins, George Mawer and Co., Agricultural Surveyors, Auctioneers and Estate Agents.

**Cattle heading home
from the Market past
The Alms Houses c.1898**

Robert Hoyes Family Butcher

This family business began trading in the 1920's, in which is now the Flea Market on the corner of Cemetery Road. Fred Johnson was a young butcher's boy in its early days, often wheeling 168 lbs. of Argentine beef from Wragby railway station on a sack barrow to the shop. A slaughter house was situated some distance behind the shop where animals were killed and later cut into joints. Mr. Hoyes had a van which enabled him to visit customers in the out lying villages. On his retirement in the early 1960's the business was carried on by Fred Johnson and his son Malcolm, later relocating to the Market Place where Gothic House is now situated.

Fred Johnson and helper Stan Burnett with Argentinean Beef 1926

Holmes Woodyard

No-one seems to know quite when and how Holmes began. Some records are available from 1809 and in 1840 John Holmes wrote *"Begin nothing without considering what the end may be"*. The company may have begun as a wheelwright business which grew and prospered, to expand the business into other timber products. It started on the present site of the Town Hall but, in 1866, the Lincoln Road premises were acquired for an outlay of £170 14s 11d. That price included the rhubarb, apple and plum trees.

In 1886, John Henry Holmes was taken on by John Holmes as a partner. But the real drive and impetus came from Annie Gadd, who married John Henry Holmes in January 1881. She was a real character. Their son was John Edward Clarke Holmes and his son was Godfrey Holmes; the last family member to be involved.

The family were strongly influenced by John Wesley and played a leading role in Wragby Methodist Church. At the 150th anniversary of the company, Mr. Godfrey Holmes said that Methodism had encouraged the family to do their utmost to develop their talents.

In 1966, with no family member to take over, the business was sold to United Africa Company (Timber) Ltd. They soon built a new sawmill and kilns. However, this very large corporation felt uncomfortable with the small firm and it was sold to G. Gruneberg (Timber and Veneers) Ltd in 1979. It became the foremost supplier of timber for sea defences and dock work.

It seems horrifying today but Holmes helped clear many pieces of woodland, for agriculture, on the big estates, particularly during the Second World War. Later the timber, oak, beech, ash, elm, sycamore, larch and spruce timber came mostly from the North of England but a shortage resulted in Holmes' turning to the use of West African wood. This was shipped into Hull and the logs were frequently eight to ten tons. Home grown timber would remain in the yard for a year or two but the west African wood was soon reduced to eight or ten feet lengths by hand with electric saws. Then they would be manoeuvred into the saw mill and cut with revolving band saws into planks and posts.

Holmes' Woodyard on Lincoln Road 1975

In the joinery shop, the range of Holmes' finished goods was vast; animal housing and feeding units of every kind, farrowing pens, tumbrils, hecks and cribs, grain drying equipment, garden sheds, boat houses, cricket pavilions and, of course, miles and miles of fencing.

Many Wragby men worked for Holmes for many years and older residents will recall Eric Campbell, Arthur Blood and Stan Hill. In 1989 the land was sold for housing and the main road into the estate was called – what else but Holmes Way.

Wragby Plastics

Godfrey Holmes was the owner of Holmes Joinery and during the Second World War, he heard that wood flour was used in the manufacture of plastics. He immediately saw an outlet for the large quantities of sawdust, which was proving to be an embarrassing waste. He bought a couple of compression moulding machines and began making combs and ashtrays in a garage. It was not until later that he realised that it was a very special type of wood flour, which was required for the plastics industry.

The company was an early entrant into the export market; some of the ashtrays were embossed with words from the Koran and sent to the Far East. It expanded rapidly and soon had machinery for compression and

Wragby Plastics 1974

injection moulding. They made puzzles, dolls house furniture, lamp standards and many other items for the toy trade.

In 1956, Wragby Plastics began its relationship with Harrison Drape, manufacturers of curtain rails. In 1969, Harrison's bought the company and new extrusion machines were put to work 24 hours a day to make various designs of the rails; Glideway, Style and Ezeglide. They also made tubing for the aerosol industry, parts for telephones and cameras as well as continuing with the toy market. In their heyday, they employed over 500 people.

In the 1960's the factory manufactured the super pencil; a writing instrument designed to meet the requirements of modern life. This was developed by the GPO for use by their telephonists. Previously each telephonist had used an average of 14 ballpoint pens a year, making a hefty bill. The production run was 140,000.

McKechnie Plastics bought Harrison's, in 1989, and Wragby Plastics became part of this large corporation; renamed as McKechnie Plastics Components –Wragby Operation. They made parts for many large companies; some of its key customers were Philips, Northern Telecom, Motorola and Polaroid. In the 1990's, their largest customer was Dyson and they made a good proportion of the vacuum cleaners.

However, the upsurge of the plastics industry in the Far East took its toll on the company, as customers found they could purchase the same parts for a fraction of the cost. Other factories in the company were in development areas and could source funding from the government. The company was closed, in 2002. Some of the staff moved to Stamford Bridge in Yorkshire but many, who had worked the company for many years, suddenly found themselves unemployed.

The factory has been demolished and Stamford Homes have nearly completed the new housing development on what was once the pride of Wragby.

E.H. Thorne (Beehives) Ltd.

Thorne's started trading in beehives and beekeeping equipment in 1920 but the story begins in 1913 with Edgar Henry Thorne, a joiner and foreman, of the Turnor Estate at Panton. Edgar started his own business of carpenter, joiner, wheelwright, painter and decorator in 1910 moving to the present site in 1920. His first contact with bees was in 1913, when the Wragby School Headmaster, Mr. Banks, who was a well known local beekeeper, asked Edgar to make him a few beehives. From this request E.H. Thorne (Beehives) Ltd was born.

Edgar purchased the corner plot at the junction of Louth Road and Silver Street from Leonard Doughty. It was a pinfold for stray cattle and sheep and cost £25. From here Edgar ran his small, thriving business; repairing carts and wagons (the building was large enough to take a typical hay wagon) painting and fencing. Mr. Banks, however, had really got Edgar hooked on bees and was Edgar's mentor, teaching him all he knew about beekeeping.

Edgar Thorne making Beehives c1949/50

In 1916, Edgar married Sarah Rowson, from a nearby village. They had two sons, Harry, born in 1918 and Leslie (Les), in 1923. Harry was not particularly interested in working with his father and took up employment selling tyres for Godfrey Holmes. Les, however, loved working with his father and the local community and bees became his hobby as well as his occupation.

At the end of the war, in 1945, Les obtained a 'B' release from the army because of his fathers failing health and link to such a vital industry. He started to take charge of the day to day running of the company which was still a painters, decorators and joiners, but Les's heart was with the bees. This side of the business was all consuming to Les and he promoted beekeeping supplies as best as he could in the difficult times just after the war.

E.H. Thorne exhibited for the first time at The Royal Show, which, at this time, was nomadic, and toured the country. The first one they went to, with much trepidation, was held at Shrewsbury. The company's stand was alongside those of Robert Lee and E.H. Taylor, the pacemakers as far as beekeeping equipment was concerned for the past 80 years or so. Naturally Thorne's were treated with derision but, at this time, there were competitions for hives and their quality of construction. Thorne's won!

The company produced its own small catalogue covering all the basic beekeeping equipment. The timber hives and frames were made at Wragby.

Edgar still controlled the purse strings and was against any type of modernisation that might be in the offing. Les had plans for a 2 hp electric motor rather than steam and he even mentioned the word 'telephone'. That was almost blasphemy to Edgar. He insisted that it was not necessary; *"I've done without one all these years and my father before me"*. A typical attitude at the time.

Thorne's continued manufacturing their beekeeping equipment alongside the expanding joinery and decorating business. Les, by now, was running a small building firm which would eventually employ over 50 staff, building quality homes and housing estates throughout Lincolnshire. The two businesses ran side by side during the 50's and 60's and modern woodworking machines were installed with compressed air rams. Then, in 1968, Thorne's purchased a wax plant from Germany, to make their own beeswax foundation sheets.

The company's expertise in a variety of fields grew and grew. It was rapidly becoming the largest manufacturer in the UK and one of the largest in Europe. Their specialist strengths were hive and frame manufacture and foundation production. To add to this, however, the company developed many plastic articles that are now commonplace in beekeeping.

In 1972, the building side of the business was sold to Hugh Bourn and Thorne's concentrated solely on beekeeping equipment. They installed more machines and created new departments to make protective clothing, smokers and extractors. In 1990 Thorne's completely gutted the inside of the building and made the only beekeeping supermarket in the UK.

**E.H. Thorne's Offices
on the Louth Road**

Exports are numerous: 800 Langstroth Hives to Oman; 2000 hives, 6000 veils and tonnes of wax to Iraq; extractors to Kuwait; National Hives to the Falklands and even queen marking kits to Antarctica (for identifying molluscs, not bees!)

In 1984 Thorne's took over their great rivals and competitors E.H. Taylor of Welwyn in Hertfordshire. The firm which once had its own railway siding, was now under the control of that insignificant firm from Wragby. In the 1990's two branches near Windsor and Dundee were opened and in 2006, a further branch was opened in North Hampshire.

For many years, E.H. Thorne looked for a new side to the business which would help the cash flow during the winter months. It was under their nose all the time – bees – beeswax – candles – candlemaking equipment. They are now the largest suppliers in the UK of moulds, wick; in fact anything for making candles.

In 1976, Paul Smith, Les's son-in-law, joined the company and is now the Managing Director and runs the company with his wife Gill. Their daughter, Rebecca (fourth generation) joined the company in 2006.

I.W. Sutton

Gentlemen's Hairdresser

Taken from an Article in *Lincolnshire Life*
By Diane Sutton - February 1984

My grandfather learnt his trade as a lather boy for his brother Walter behind the brick-arched facade of William Sutton's second Drapers, Tailors and Outfitter's shop on the south-east side of Wragby Market Place. The cut-throat razors would be wiped on squares of newspaper, and on Saturday nights my grandfather would prepare 50 of these. In 1908, Walter was charging a penny a shave.

In July 1911 my grandfather opened his own hairdresser's shop next door to the Post Office and remained there, looking out into the Market Place, until 1961. During the First War, when grandfather was a signaler in France, Walter worked in the shop two or three nights a week in order to keep the trade going for his return. This was the longest break my grandfather took from his work. It was only after the First War that the shop became firmly established, not only as a place where men could have their hair cut, be shaved and buy tobacco, but also as a popular meeting place where they could relax, chat and joke among themselves. It may have been this latter social function—which is the one most commented on by anyone who knew the shop—which kept grandfather cutting short-back-and-sides for 50 years.

**Market Place c1932 showing the Post Office, Sutton's Drapery and Sutton's Hairdresser
(The little tent in the middle sold strawberries)**

During this time (at least the years my father knew it) the shop hardly altered. Two wooden benches rested on the worn red-tiled floor. Opposite was the shaving basin and an electric copper kettle which heated water needed for shaves. In between stood the wooden hairdressing chair, and in the back corner another which was moved to the basin for the Saturday night shaves. The counter and walls were stacked with tobacconists goods (including clay pipes in the early days) and combs, shampoos, haircreams, soaps and toothbrushes.

In later years cosmetics, perfumes and Toni's home perms were added. Yellowing photographs of Wragby's football teams, from as early as 1912, hung on the walls together with advertisements for cigarettes and tobacco.

To begin with, however, grandfather did not sell tobacco as this was Walter's prerogative, and to stock it would have competed with his grocer's shop. The men, therefore, bought their cigarettes and thick twist there. The latter was described by my grandmother as a 'solid piece of black like Spanish, which came in a block and they would cut bits off to put in their pipes and smoke it.....horrible.' Later, when he did begin to sell tobacco, grandfather would order it directly from Wills at Bristol or Players at Nottingham and supply some of it wholesale to the Ivy Club in the Market Place, the Wayside Cafe at Bullington, and to an old lady down the Langton Road who sold tobacco and cigarettes to the farm people. During the Second War, he kept some under the counter for regular customers.

The shop was open six days a week, though Wednesday was eventually chosen as Wragby's half-day. Grandfather opened at nine in the morning but closing times were variable as there was no shutting-up time; if people kept coming , you kept open. He would frequently go back after tea and not return until eight or nine in the evening. During WWII, airmen stationed at Wickenby, would have their hair cut in the evenings when they were free and so Grandfather stayed open. By this time most men shaved themselves, but earlier in the century they went to the hairdressers one a week.

Saturday nights were still the busiest up until grandfather's retirement, with both chairs in use as customers were shaved ready for Sunday. Walt Dixon was grandfather's lather boy for many years and helped on Saturday evenings when he would lather the customers over the basin in the corner. This drained into a bucket which had to be emptied round the back of the block in the Post Office yard, and this tedious job was often left to my father on the occasions he helped in the shop.

Waiting for a Haircut

**Frank Wright, Joe Dixon,
Harold Woodward, John Priestley
And Charlie Hickson**

Staying open 'just to suit the customers' may have brought more trade, but had its disadvantages as Frank Seely remembers: 'On Saturday nights it was so aggravating because Mr. Kilmister used to come up .. . to our house in the Market Place for about quarter to nine and then we would adjourn to the Adam and Eve. We went across for granddad and there were these bloomin' fellows, who could have come in ages before arriving for a shave, at about nine or so, and granddad was too polite with them. There was one old boy who, when we wanted to go anywhere footballing in George Scott's old solid-tyred bus, to Bishop Norton or Kelsey - somewhere like that, just as it was time to load up the bus he would come in for a shave - on purpose! Everybody was sitting in the bus until he was shaved'. It seems that grandfather could also close to suit himself, when occasion demanded.

Saturday night was also the busiest, as far as the number of gossipers went. Regulars, such as Charlie Hickson and Harold, used to come just to sit and have their legs pulled. These two were a 'bit simple' and worked as farm labourers. Charlie fencing and ditching at Kilmister's farm, Harold (older and less capable) bussing from Atkin's farm at East Barkwith, where one of his jobs was to look after the poultry. The men in the shop reckoned that Charlie would mark the end of his ditch with a stick so that he knew where to start from the next day. Many people in the district went to Wragby on Saturday evenings to shop, have a shave and go for a drink; it was their night out. They would go to grandfather for their cigarettes and tobacco, often stopping for a chat, and the shop would be full of smoke and talk and laughter.

Such activity was not confined to Saturday nights, however. A few gossipers gathered their every morning, including `the rather dim-witted and more-or-less retired', the latter being well entertained by the joking and leg-pulling which went on. Mr. Dove and Mr. Seely (whose office was opposite the shop) also used to go over during the day for a chat. As the *Market Rasen Mail* reported in 1961: `If there was ever a bit of business to discuss, it might be more correct to call a meeting but so much easier for the elders to gather unofficially in the little hairdresser's shop. . . . Here too, long before the Town Hall was thought of, was a sort of unofficial town parlour with congenial surroundings and companionship.

My father used to look after the shop when grandmother and grandfather went on holiday. The regulars spent their days elsewhere and, only dealing with sales of goods, he found the days interminably long so gave the shop its annual spring-clean, dusting the shelves and reddening the tiled floor.

Grandfather's busiest working hours were in the evenings when the customers had time for a haircut after finishing their own work. He would often return home exhausted, particularly during the Second World War with its added number of airmen's haircuts. Still charging 1 s 6d for a haircut in the late 1950's when it would cost much more elsewhere, it seems that grandfather was not concerned with making vast profits. Nor did the work itself hold much variety, but this was provided by the men who gathered there.

The shop's central position in the Market Place, the customers' frequent wait, and the fact that the job gave grandfather the opportunity to chat with each person as he was cutting his hair promoted the shop's development as a meeting place. A 50 year period in such a position gave him an almost unique status as observer and participant in a way of life that, at least beyond his shop window, was rapidly changing.

Dove & Son

General and Furnishing Ironmongers

The Dove family came to Wragby in the early 1820's from the Northampton area and in 1826, William Dove was carrying on the business of plumber and glazier. The Ironmonger shop was established around 1850 on the west side of the Market Place where the Corn Dolly cafe now stands. On an invoice of 1895, they sold builders materials, farming implements, chaff and turnip cutters, nails, galvanised netting, kitchen

Dove & Son Market Place 1913

111

ranges, cast iron guttering and galvanised roof sheeting. Also sold were household appliances such as bedsteads and mattresses, wringers for washing, sewing machines, perambulators and many other every-day items.

In 1917, with the motor car in more general use, Dove's had moved to the east side of the Market Place, had built a garage and were selling petrol in cans to local car owners and passing motorists. It was situated in front of The old Red Lion pub, now the CB shop and public toilets.

In 1882, Charles Dove was recorded as being a tinner, brazier and ironmonger, as was Wedd Henry Dove & Son in 1895. In the 1930's Albert Burrell Dove was running the business as a motor engineering workshop. He was also a radio and cycle dealer.

As more cars, vans and small lorries began to pass through Wragby in the late 1930's, Dove's acquired six petrol pumps. Three of these were hand wound to serve petrol and three were electric, they consisted of Shell, RP, Cleveland, National Benzol, Esso and Power. For the duration of the war the army requisitioned the three electric pumps to supply petrol to the army vehicles stationed in Wragby and the surrounding district.

Dove & Son, Market Place after a heavy snow fall February 1947

In the post war years, business was good, with regular customers including Wragby Plastics and Holmes Woodyard. Dove's also had a busy Calor Gas round, delivering cylinders to neighbouring villages. The old Pentecostal Church which was behind the bus stop on the Lincoln road belonged to Mr. Dove and in the early 1950's he ran a successful sack hire agency, belonging to Chisholm, Fox and Gamer. This enterprise provided local farmers with sacks for corn as early combine harvesters were only geared to load bags. As time passed, the much larger combines held a ton of corn which was dispatched into a waiting trailer, so ending the sack hire business.

Alf Shaw, a schoolboy refugee from Hull, who came to live with the Dove family during the war, stayed on and worked as the motor engineer until Mr. Dove retired in 1970. Mr. Dove then sold the garage to Ted and Eileen Green, from East Barkwith, who carried on the motor engineering, and also M.O.T testing. Petrol sales were stopped by the council in the mid 70's as the pump lines crossed the footpath proving an inconvenience to the public. In January 1983, Ted Green sold the garage to Bernard and Irene Andrews who continued with car repairs and maintenance until 1986. The garage was demolished on 21st November 1986 to make way for the public toilets and C.B shop.

Market Place 1962

Forest Lodge Guns

The shop, in Louth Road, opened in 1987, with the intention of establishing an "old fashioned gun shop" rather than a department store type of operation. Ten years ago the premises were extended, just about doubling the shop size and a further extension is now planned. Three partners, Colin, Carole and Matt Comins run the business and in addition to selling and repairing guns, offer high quality outdoor clothing, binoculars, fly fishing tackle etc., for the shooting and country fraternity. Colin and Matt are qualified deer stalkers and travel to Finland annually to take part in stalking moose. Colin started a Clay Pigeon Club in 1986. It was originally at Bardney Dairies but has now moved to Gordon Blakey's Farm, Sotby. The club is still active although Colin and Matt are no longer members, due to business pressures.

Bradshaw & Son

John Bradshaw was born around 1853 in Chapel St. Leonards, and in 1871 became an apprentice wheelwright in Hogsthorpe. He married in 1877 and went to live in Louth, employed as a joiner in 1881 having already started a family. Sometime between 1885 and 1889 the family moved to Wragby and Mr. Bradshaw began trading as a Grocer, Drapers, Provision and Wine Merchant. His shop was in Church Street opposite what was the old National School and is now the Youth Centre and Sports Hall.

By 1891 John had five children, the eldest boy being William, aged 12; they had one servant and an apprentice grocer. Business must have been good as by 1901 William had become a fully fledged grocer. The name of the business was changed, in 1913, from Bradshaw's to Bradshaw & Son. John's youngest son, Sid, had taken over the business and was still trading when he retired in the 1960's and the shop was closed for good. According to records, John Bradshaw died in 1933 aged 80 years.

The shop, being adjacent to the school, became the local tuck-shop for pupils and, before the advent of Supermarkets, supplied the village with most everyday items from food, wine and drapery to black and white film with developing and printing. In 1932 it was possible to buy three gents shirts for 4/11d – 75p in today's money; Whisky was 4/- a bottle, eggs 20 for 1/- and Woodbine cigarettes were 2d for 10! Wednesday was early closing day when the shop closed at 1 o'clock prompt.

The shop was demolished in the 1970's and a private house was built on the site.

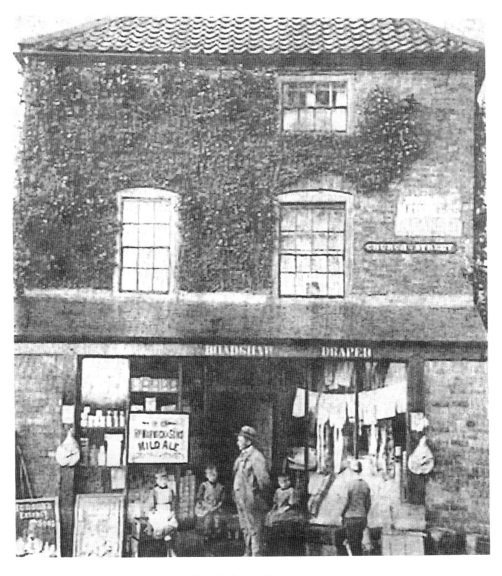

Bradshaw Drapers

C & J Hauton

C & J Hauton was established in 1961 by father and son Cyril and John Hauton Their first vehicles were 10 ton Bedford TK Tippers which they used to transport corn from local farmers to Preston Farmers in Preston, Lancashire. They also did work for DMT and Denby's of Lincoln.

Cyril and John Hauton with their Bedford Lorries at Wragby 1960's

Cyril died in 1972 and it was around this time that there was a slump in the haulage industry in this country, so John decided to branch out into European transport. This took him to countries such as Italy, Austria and Greece. After a couple of years John became more adventurous; he was offered work transporting goods to the Middle East, and John began going as far afield as Saudi Arabia, where he once delivered carpets to the Jeddah Palace, home of the King of Saudi Arabia.

The business expanded to the extent that it was operating seven trucks in the Middle East which was not easy work. The journey involved travelling through nine countries, dealing with nine different currencies and the associated border controls. It was often a treacherous journey and meant passing through the Eastern Bloc Communist countries of Bulgaria, Hungary, Romania, Czechoslovakia and Yugoslavia, each with its own challenging terrain and culture.

Work also took the business to Iraq, Iran, Kuwait and Turkey. Once while making a delivery to a development in Baghdad, John was approached by an English contract worker who had spotted the 'Wragby' on the door of the lorry. He proceeded to tell John how he regularly visited Don Wells' Fish and Chip shop when home on leave!

By 1982 the work was no longer as attractive as it had been to begin with and over the next few years the firm gradually downsized. At the same time Michael, John's eldest son, left school and began work in the family business, helping with the day to day running of the business and vehicle maintenance. After passing his car driving test, Michael worked for DMT and Wragby Plastics on 7½-ton vehicles until gaining his Class 1 licence.

John's youngest son, Robert, joined the firm in 1987 and followed in Michael's footsteps transporting goods for Wragby Plastics. Michael was then driving an articulated lorry following his father out to the Middle East.

With the guidance of their mother Ann, Michael and Robert took over the running of the business after the death of their father, John, in 1992. For several years Michael continued to work on the continent, while Robert gained his Class 1 licence and established the business back in the UK contracting to companies around Immingham and Grimsby delivering imported goods.

C & J Hauton continues to operate with Michael and Robert, both now working in the UK with 44 ton vehicles delivering a wide variety of goods the length and breadth of the country.

Market Place 1967

New Buildings by Elaine Dixon - 29th May 1964
At the plastics Factory they are building some new offices. Arthur Clark is building them. There will be a drawing office a wage office and some more.

MARKETS and SHOWS

Markets

The earliest markets held in Wragby go back 786 years to 1221 when the Lord of the manor, William de Ros (later Roos) was granted permission to hold a weekly Thursday market by Henry III 'in his minority'. The Sheriff of Lincoln was duly notified of this, as was the custom of the day. As stated previously, it appears that the permissions were applied for on a yearly basis 'until the King came of age'. In 1223 the day of the market was changed to a Wednesday – again 'until the King came of age'. In 1227 the Sheriff of Lincolnshire was ordered to exempt the market from the general prohibition of markets and fairs raised during the King's minority.

(King Henry III was born in 1207 and was crowned King when aged 9, in 1216, but did not rule as King until he was 25 years old. He reigned for 56 years and died in 1272.)

The markets must have been a great success because in 1384 Beatrice, widow of Thomas de Roos of Hamelock, Knight, was still holding a Wednesday market. It is therefore interesting that George Villiers, Duke of Buckingham, cousin and councillor of the King, obtained a charter from Charles II in 1669 permitting the holding of a weekly Thursday market and three annual fairs to be held on 24th February, 18th September and 8th October. It also granted permission to hold 'Courts of Piepowder' (*An ancient court of record in England, formerly incident to every fair and market, of which the steward of him who owned or had the toll was the judge*).

It becomes obvious, searching the records, that apart from the Thursday market the number and dates of the fairs were not adhered to. The directory of 1792 acknowledges the Thursday market and states 'here are two considerable fairs for cattle on Ascension and Michaelmas Days'. *(Ascension Day is 40 days after Easter and Michaelmas Day is 29th September)* By 1828 the Ascension Day fair was for sheep and the Michaelmas Day for cattle only.

The Cattle Market - 1966

This continued until 1861 when the Directory lists an extra day for the cattle fair on 28th September with the other days remaining the same. It also states that the Market House was not used as often since the coming of the railway but the market was still held on Thursdays. By 1872 the Market House was not used at all and the Thursday market 'was of trifling consequence'. The market was in abeyance by 1885 and only two fairs were being held, those for cattle on 1st May and 28th and 29th September.

Sheep Fair

Prior to World War I we find that the Thursday market is extinct. Fairs for cattle were now held on 1st May and 28th September, with a fair for foals and sheep being held on 29th September. The Market House now housed the Fire Engine. Other sources tell us that butter and eggs were still being sold in the Market Place during the early part of the twentieth century.

The last cattle market was held in 1979 and today the remnants of the cattle pens can still be seen at the rear of the Co-op building in the area called Fairfield. Nothing remains of the sheep markets as they were held on the Lincoln Road where Priory Grange stands today. The horse fairs were held in the Market Place,

Wragby Horse Fair

as the picture shows, leaving no lasting reminder. Today we only have a Christmas Market early in December organised by the Uniformed Headquarters Management Committee.

Shows

The Wragby Floral and Horticultural Society was established in 1873 and held their first ever Flower Show the following year. Unfortunately not a lot is known about the early years as the only programme found for that period is dated 1892 which was the 19th annual show and was held on Thursday 28th July. The Show called 'Wragby Horticulture & Cottage Gardening Exhibition' was held on the vicarage grounds, courtesy of the Rev. H. Bolland and Mr. J. Weightman. *(In those days the vicarage was the house on the corner of the Horncastle and Louth Roads and the grounds covered the area which now holds the primary school, swimming pool and town hall.)*

There were three sections of horticulture and flowers; one for Cottagers, defined as 'a person whose sole livelihood is gained either as an Agricultural Labourer not occupying more than ten acres of Land, or Mechanic not in business for himself; a section for Amateurs within the radius specified in the rules – ten miles from Wragby; the last section 'Open to all Gardeners and all Lincolnshire'. A special section – a Bouquet of Wild Flowers – was for School children under the age of 12 years.

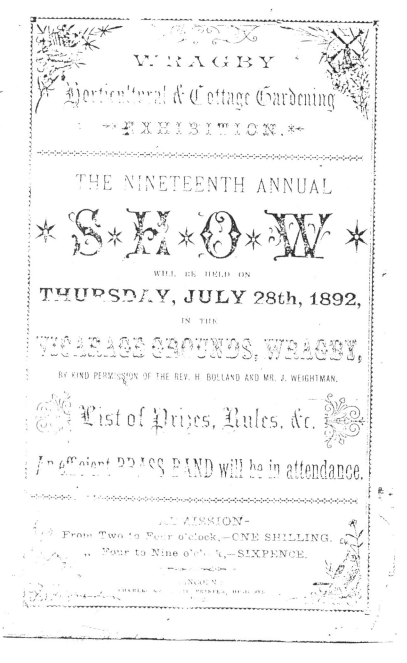

In addition to the Horticulture and Flowers exhibits there was a programme of other events including Driving and Jumping, games on horseback including a Cigarette and Umbrella Race and a Boot Race. The games were not just confined to horses as there was also a class for Musical Chairs on Bicycles. A brass band was in attendance and a Lawn Tennis tournament was also held on the day.

The financial details of the Society make interesting reading as the balance sheet for 1891 shows. The Show was open from 2 o'clock in the afternoon until 9 o'clock in the evening and the entrance fee was 1/- until 4 o'clock and thereafter 6d. Despite providing good and varied entertainment for the public the Show made very little profit having to take money from the reserve fund to balance the books.

BALANCE SHEET FOR 1891.

RECEIPTS.	£	s	d	DISBURSEMENTS.	£	s	d
Members' Contributions	54	16	0	Prize Money	47	18	0
Gate Money	41	3	10	Tents, Band, Sports, Printing, &c.	60	2	2
Tea and Sundries	17	16	5	Sundries	6	12	4
	£113	16	3				
Balance from Reserve Fund	0	16	3				
	£114	12	6		£114	12	6

The Society had 16 Patrons/Patronesses, a President, 4 Vice Presidents, a Committee of 33 and a list of Subscribers, that reads like a veritable who's who of Lincolnshire. Included were Edmund Turnor, Esq., Lady Mary Turnor, and the Right Honourable Edward Heneage M.P. Although Lady Eleanor Heneage was Patroness she was not mentioned on the list of Subscribers. The majority were from Lincolnshire, covering the area from Spalding to Louth, but one gentleman listed was from Chislehurst, Kent!

The Twentieth Annual Show held the following year included Long and High Jumping competitions and a novelty competition as well as the previously mentioned events. The band that year was the Lincoln Malleable Ironworks prize band, which played throughout the day and provided the music for dancing in the evening. The Show closed with a brilliant display of fireworks. The organisers were even thoughtful enough to have the times of the last trains to Lincoln and Louth printed in the programme.

By 1889 the Directories tell us that as well as the Flower Show in July a Foal Show was now held in September, although by 1896 this had changed to August. In 1913 the Show was held in a field on the East side of Silver Street because Mr. Clarke was the secretary. No programme has come to light for that year but we know that the usual programme of events took place along with a decorated bicycle competition and tug of war games. Once again the day ended with a large firework display. This was to be the last Show before the outbreak of WWI and for the next four years the Show was held in abeyance.

The Show started up again in 1918 and according to the 1919 Directory, both the Flower and the Foal Shows were held annually in July.

The 44th Annual Show, 1921, was once again held in the Vicarage and adjoining grounds. The events had again increased and so had the admission prices. These were now 2/- up to 4 o'clock and 1/6 afterwards. Dancing was to take place at 7 p.m. with the Flower Show closing at 7-30 p.m. as can be seen on the programme below.

Sadly 1929 saw the last show of the era. The following years were marred by political instabilities, a high level of unemployment, government financial misfortunes and regal upheavals. Then came the uncertainties of the immediate pre-war years followed by the war. In 1945, it had been 16 years since the last Wragby Show and it was to be a total of 54 years after that 'final show' before its resurrection as the Wragby & District Show.

The rebirth came about quite by chance from a casual remark. In May 1983, Harry Bruntlett was buying cigarettes in West Torrington and during his conversation with Gordon Allen, the shopkeeper, remarked that it was a pity that Wragby didn't have a show of its own anymore. Gordon mentioned it to Frank Dickinson, who got in touch with Harry. They arranged a meeting and invited local people to attend. On the night 17 people turned up and as a result a committee was formed. George Woolgar wrote a letter which was published in a local paper; he gave a potted history of the previous shows, mentioned the notable sponsors of that time and asked for financial support to re-establish the show. As events have proved, the letter was obviously successful.

Within five months the committee had put on a Show that attracted over a thousand visitors and was considered, at the time, to be one of the finest small shows in the area. It is little short of miraculous that in such a short time they had arranged trade stands, a Gymkhana, a horticultural show and the main ring attraction of a sheep dog display by the Young Farmers. Also arranged was a parade of vintage cars headed by Dave Hoban and his formula 2 racing car. Among the side displays were a model aeroplane and railway displays, a pet show and among many other displays, for the first time, a goat show.

The Show has continued with this format to the present day, recently changing its name to 'Wragby Show & Country Fayre' but still know locally as 'The Wragby Show'. The animal section has been expanded to include agricultural horses, cattle, sheep, rare breeds and, of course, goats. The flower and horticulture exhibits still follow the same format as of old, however the main ring attractions have become more adventurous and have included motorbike stunt teams.

Sadly, the Gymkhana games and fancy dress have had to be discontinued because there has not been enough interest or support. The Show Jumping section now includes In Hand hunter and horse classes and for the past few years the committee has managed to persuade the Battle of Britain Memorial Flight to give a fly past by one of their aircraft in the late afternoon of Show Day. The Charity and Trade stands have proved popular additions as have the vintage car and stationary engine sections.

The 25th Show, since its revival, was held in 2007 and is still proving to be a very popular event. Unfortunately the Foot and Mouth outbreaks of 2001 and 2007 severely hampered the format but the committee still managed to put on record breaking shows.

When you look back at the number of committee members and subscribers of the early Shows it is remarkable that the present Show Committee can present a full packed day of entertainment with an average compliment of 12 members. This is mainly due to their dedicated organisational skills, hard work and also to the friends and helpers of the Show who work on the day itself. Funds are raised by advertisements in the programme, trade stands and by the generous support of their many sponsors.

All in all Wragby Show & Country Fayre is a great day out and, as the profits go to various charities each year, can be highly recommended. The benefactors of the 2007 Show are Queen's Park School, Lincoln; The Nomad Trust; Wragby Youth Club and Disability Lincs Wragby.

**Sue Cosgrove receiving The Herring Tropy
for Supreme Champion from President Mike Perkins**

Wragby Show & Country Fayre 2007

No Limitz Jnr. Motorbike Stunt Team

BUILDINGS OF NOTE

The Old Bakehouse

The bakehouse and shop, in the Market Place, were purchased for £375 by George Mawer at the sale of the Turnor estate in 1917. The property was sold on in 1918 to George Clark Musson whose father, Joseph Edward Musson owned a working mill in Minting.

The business was run by George's wife Annie and a bread 'round' was established. Supplies were initially delivered to homes throughout the area by horse and cart and, later, in an early model Ford van. The bakery was in full operation throughout the Second World War.

Musson's Bakery Market Place

When Annie died in 1955, her son, Joseph Edward Musson (named after his grandfather), took over the business, helped by his wife Auria. 'Musson's Bakery' became well known for it's plum bread, swiss rolls and teacakes and was a regular stopping off point for visitors passing through to the coast.

The bakery closed in 1962 when the baker at the time, Cyril Greenfield, became ill. Wonderloaf, a market leader at the time, bought the bread round. George and Annie's daughter, Joyce, ran the shop for a further two years selling bread supplied by Wonderloaf. The shop finally closed in 1964 and the premises became home to Joyce and her daughter, Fiona. For a short period of time, the house was named 'Musson House'.

Fiona continues to live in the family home which is now called 'The Old Bakehouse', along with her husband and son, Stewart and Oliver Smith.

The Windmill

The sail mill can be seen on the Bardney Road and was built in 1831 by a Mr. Ingledew, a millwright from Gainsborough. It was wind driven until 1892 and powered by wind and oil engine to 1903, when it became solely driven by an oil engine.

The first owner was Mr. J. Clark. It had six sails, which attained 32hp, driving four pairs of grinding stones and other machinery within the tower. It was constructed of local Wragby brick with lime and mortar from the Panton sand pits. Henry Mawer took over the ownership of the mill in 1867 and Preston Farmers closed the mill completely on 30th April, 1997.

The mill was twice struck by lightning and we believe that this caused the loss of its sails. Now in private ownership, the mill has been restored to a pristine condition, albeit without sails.

Wragby Mill in Full Sail

The Gate House

Situated on Wire Hill Lane, the Gate House, was the home of various gate keepers who manned the railway level crossing. The occupants, as we know them, are mentioned below.

John Clark: The first to occupy Gate House and was employed by the Railway as a Plate Layer. According to the 1901 census Susannah Clark was the gate keeper. The Clark family lived here for 50 years.

Mr. Johnson: He arrived about 1926 and a gate opened the crossing for five years. After Mr. Johnson left it became an automatic pole opening crossing. Apparently Mr. Johnson's son was a policeman.

Mr. Dennis: He occupied the house from around 1935, staying 23 plus years. He left in 1958.

From 1958 to 1962 the Gatehouse was derelict.

Mr. Taylor: In residence from 1962 to 1973

Jim Sutherland: Margaret and Jim bought the house in 1973 and have lived there, ever since. The house was put up for sale in 2007.

The above information was recently obtained from Jim Sutherland, who assumed the Gate House was built by the Railway Company prior to Mr. Clark's occupancy.

Working back from 2007, taking into account the periods of occupancy of the Gate House, we arrive back to 1876. Records state the line was opened in December 1876 by the Louth-Company, which was bought during 1872 by the Great Northern Railway.

The Gate House

Beech House

It is not known when Beech House, on Silver Street, was built but the ground floor has three stone walls, two at the sides and one across the middle of the house Some of the stones are shaped so they may have been stolen during the dissolution of the abbeys. Perhaps it was once a blacksmith's shop.   On the gable end, the date of 1717 can be clearly seen. It is assumed that the house is named after the beautiful old gnarled beech tree in the garden.

We know that a Mr. Moody lived in the house in the early 1830's.   The two old bills below were found in the beam over the inglenook fireplace, when the house was renovated in the 1980's.

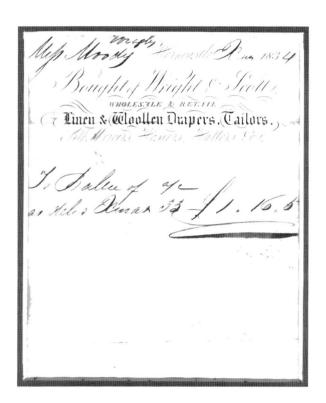
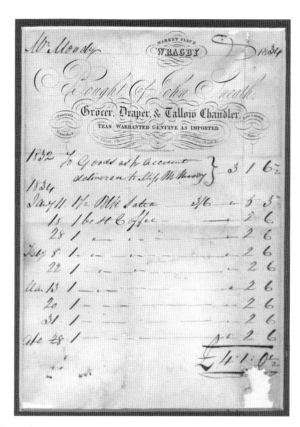

It is unlikely that many people would get two years credit today!

It is thought that Mr. Moody was Mr. Enos Moody, described as an attorney or lawyer. He lived in Beech House with his wife Jane and an 85 year old lady called Elizabeth Moody (perhaps his grandmother). According to the 1841 census, Samuel Bolton (14), an agricultural labourer, Mary Hill (20) and Ann Wallis (15), both farm servants and Henry Foster, aged just 10, who were also in residence there.

In 1881, three ladies lived in Beech House; Ellen Campbell (50) and her two nieces, Alvina and Kate Weightman, aged 21 and 18 respectively. These ladies were clearly of independent means as they had a housemaid, a domestic cook and a coachman.

The first of two veterinary surgeons lived there in 1891. Fred Spencer was 36 and is also described as a farmer and an insurance agent. He lived with his wife, Martha (37) and their daughter Ida (2) and just two servants – a groom and a general domestic.

In 1901, Dr. Robert William Clarke was in residence. He was a widower and lived with his sister Marion with just one servant.   He married again and the couple had two daughters.   On the outbreak of World War 1, he joined the Lincolnshire Yeomanry, receiving a commission as a veterinary lieutenant.   The huge old beech tree in the garden has a horseshoe fixed to it and there are many small holes around it.   The story is that Dr. (by now Captain) Clarke practised his shooting skills from the back door – aiming for the horseshoe. He served for two years, travelling through the Mediterranean, finally arriving in Egypt. Here he was struck down with a fatal attack of dysentery. He died in August 1916.

Beech House was sold, in 1917, with the remainder of the Panton Estate. It was bought by Mr. Thomas Doughty for £875.00. It is believed that an appendix operation was performed on Mr. Doughty, in the drawing room.

In 1930, Beech House was sold to a Mr. Robert Bygott, when Mr. Doughty had built and moved into Navarino, on the corner of Louth Road and Silver Street. In 1953, Mr. Bygott, then aged 90 and Gillian Thorne, aged one (who now lives in Beech House), both laid foundation stones for the Wragby Town Hall.

Later in the 1950's, Beech House was purchased by the Stubbs family, two brothers and one sister. Many Wragby residents will remember Roy Stubbs who continued to live in Wragby for many years. In 1981, Gill and Paul Smith purchased Beech House.

Beech House 1917

Town Hall

A very brief history of the Town Hall is set out in the Souvenir programme which, in 1979, marked the Silver Jubilee Celebration of the opening.

In 1929 several Wragby men formed a Minstrel Group with the idea of raising money to build a hall in Wragby. The War intervened, and it was in 1948 that representatives of the Wragby organisations met to decide if there was once again interest in building a hall. Such was the interest that a committee was formed and fund-raising events commenced, in particular concerts and other events in The Chalet.

The Hall was built by Mr. Leslie Thorne and stands on grounds, purchased at a modest price from the Church Commissioners, which once formed part of the Vicarage garden. The original building cost approximately £4000 and was finally opened on Saturday, 17th July, 1954, a very wet day

Mr. G.A. Kilmister, Chairman of the Town Hall Building Committee, passed on the following message: *"A page has been turned in the history of Wragby. My first thoughts are of many thanks to all of those who have worked so hard and given so freely; from the grand old lady of 92 and a certain gentleman of 93 who have made their contribution, to the small child who will, this afternoon, be on parade and be so proud of her fancy dress. As your Chairman, I am pleased to say that I have never had a refusal for any request for service, kind or money. The many helpers are too numerous to mention."*

**Mr. Alwyn Mawer Laying the First Brick
to the Town Hall in 1953**

A letter from Mr. D. Wilkinson-Fox, Chairman of the Town Hall Management Committee, read:-

"This is your Town Hall, built by your own efforts and with your own money, without financial help from the Government or other sources. That is something to be proud of, an achievement to be regarded with admiration.

Now that the Building Committee have achieved their first objective, the job of running the Town Hall will be the responsibility of the Management Committee. All organisations, clubs and similar bodies have been invited to nominate their representatives to sit on this Committee, as it has already begun to function.

We want your Town Hall to be used often; that will make it easier the task of maintaining it - but there is another reason.

This being your Town Hall, we want to ensure that the people of Wragby, Langton and Goltho use it on every possible occasion. We want to see the Town Hall as the centre of social activity of a recreational nature. That is why you built it. Help us to see your object carried out. Above all USE the Town Hall. Don't let it become a museum, a pleasant building, that people look at but don't use. Don't be shy of asking about bookings and fees. These have been especially reduced for local bodies, so that they can meet there whenever they want. Book dates with the Secretary (Mr. Bones, the School House, Wragby) and talk about costs with the Treasurer (Mr. J.P. Sutton, Rasen Road, Wragby)."

The opening began with the fancy dress for all ages and, after the official Opening Ceremony by Godfrey Holmes Esq., a short service was conducted by Rev. Wilkinson-Fox and the Methodist Minister, Rev. A. P. Hadwen. This was followed by a full programme which included a comic dog show, tug o' war, many stalls and sideshows, a grand concert and dance in the new Town Hall from 9 p.m. to midnight.

Although the original aim of providing a Town Hall had been met, the new committee was not content to sit still. The stage had been shelved because of lack of funds and the kitchens were proving too small to cope. A scheme was adopted to extend the kitchens with an additional committee room and bar. Although this put the committee into further debt it did not dampen their enthusiasm or vision and this stage was completed in 1960.

Two years later, the Committee had the opportunity to purchase the area of land behind the Town Hall, then known as The Park.   At that time Lindsey County Council was looking for a site for a new school. By selling a portion of the land to them, the Committee was able to clear all its debts and have money in hand to develop the rest of The Park as a children's playground and tennis courts.   The play area was opened in 1968 and the tennis courts in 1969.

The First Town Hall Committee 1954
Back :   Mrs. Edith Wilkinson, Mr. Ken How, Mrs. Seely, Jack Potter. Stan Hill, Ernest Wright,
Miss Ella Mawer, Mrs. E. Thorne, Eddie Robinson, Duncan Boyd, Billy Mawer, Sid Bradshaw
Roy Shuttleworth, Tommy Lockton and Les Thorne
Seated: Mr. George Kilmister, Mary Bradshaw, Frank Seely, Mrs. Dennis

From that time income has been generated by hiring the rooms and supplemented by money-making schemes.   These began with dances, then a village cinema and finally bingo, which is still going strong.

The next project was to add a stage and dressing rooms to the west end of the existing building at a cost of £12000 and have the hall wired up for stage lighting, all completed 1974/5.   At that time demand for the hall was still growing with sometimes three or four functions a day.   Wragby Players used it regularly and besides parties, jumble sales and dances, the hall had regular bookings for bingo, whist drives, chiropody clinic, classes for local handicapped people, keep fit classes for the elderly and the Darby and Joan club.

More recently the Town Hall Committee were successful in obtaining a National Lottery Grant for the complete refurbishment of the Town Hall and playground.

Standing still is something the hall has never done and let us hope that the first Chairman's plea is honoured, *"Above all USE the Town Hall. Don't let it become a museum, a pleasant building, that people look at but don't use."*

Parochial Library and Reading Room

In an unusual gesture for a Lord of the Manor, Christopher Turnor gave the upper floors of the tenement of shops, on the east side of the Market Place, to the community, free of rent, to establish a Parochial Library and Reading Room. This happened in 1856 and was for the benefit of the working men and others.

The Library contained a number of books from 1118 in 1872 to over 1800 in 1919. It also held a variety of London and Country newspapers. It was well supported by subscriptions and the proceeds from lectures given in the winter months in the latter half of the 1800's graduating to entertainments in the early 1900's.

Coat of Arms above the entrance door

Initially it was in the control of the Vicar but in 1885 Mr. J. Holmes was the Librarian with Mr. Wedd Henry Dove joining him as Honourable Secretary in 1889. From 1896 to 1912 Mr. William Atkinson and Mr. Joseph Hinds Robinson were listed as Librarian and Honourable Secretary respectively. Mr. Atkinson was again listed as Librarian in 1913 with Mr. Wedd Henry Dove again as Honourable Secretary. Change occurred in 1919 when the Librarian was Mr. William Hunter and Honourable Secretary was Mr. George Cottingham.

It is not known when the Reading Room was closed but it has now been turned into four independent flats, privately owned.

Alms Houses

Sir Edmund Turnor built a hospital* in 1697 to house six clergymen's widows and six other poor and aged persons, widow or widower. A chapel was built adjoining the houses with an augmentation of £40 per annum to the vicarage for prayers to be read in it twice a day. The chapel was consecrated with great ceremony by Bishop Gardiner, the then Bishop of Lincoln, in 1697.

Alms Houses, Turnor Square c1908

(The term hospital was used in that period to define establishments where the poor could be housed and not in the medical sense that we know today. It was only later that the term Alms Houses came into effect.)

When Sir Edmund died in 1708 he bequeathed an endowment of £100 per year rent charge out of the manor of Wragby and other estates. This endowment was to be dispersed as follows: £40 per annum to the Vicar for performing Divine Service in the chapel; £5 to each of the widows of poor clergy; £3 6s 8d to each of the poor lay person and £10 to be set aside for the reparation of the building.

The houses were rebuilt in 1840, in the gothic style, at a cost of £1950 out of funds which had accumulated over many years from the unapplied income. The chapel was deemed unnecessary due to the close proximity of the newly built church. They were further improved in 1872 at an outlay of £238 and comprise 12 tenements forming three sides of a square.

From the Directories: *The poor widows have also £5 each annually from the interest of £1000 left by the late Mrs. Yard, wife of a former vicar and vested in the 3% Consols. The poor parishioners also have the following yearly doles: £2 10s as interest of £20 left by Lady Grantham and £20 by Mrs. Jane Wells and two other donors; 10s left by William Watson in 1776 out of land called Well Close and 16s as interest of £20 left by John Harrison and the Rev. Samuel Bradshaw.*

From 1861 to 1919 the payment was 25s to the clergy widows and 16s 8d to the lay widows per quarter with donations of coals and clothing and a payment to the vicar of £40 per year.

The alms houses were again enlarged in 1907 at a cost of £209 and in 1908 at a further cost of £190 both taken out of unappropriated pension funds. At that point all further work stopped. It wasn't until 1959, when an article appeared in the local paper, that people realised the poor conditions in the alms houses. The article drew the attention to the contrasts of 'modern' traffic passing through Wragby and the state of the alms houses interiors despite their outward charm. In one house coal was kept under the stairs; in others there was no pantry, no bathroom, no bath, and no kitchen sink.

Shortly afterwards the alms houses underwent a complete renovation and modernisation and was rededicated by the Rt. Rev. Kenneth Riches, Bishop of Lincoln. Apparently there had been a full scheme proposed in 1948 at an estimated cost of £2000 that never matured. The renovations had finally cost over £10,000, £3000 of which came from Horncastle Rural District Council in the form of a grant. The 12 original houses had been converted into ten and now had modern bathrooms, toilets, kitchens, heating and electrical appliances.

Today the old rule still applies; the alms houses are for the widows of clergy and lay widows or widowers. They are still run by Trustees but in accordance with modern traditions via a Managing Agent.

Alms Houses 1999

The Workhouse

Laws relating to the problem of dealing with the poor had been in force since the 14th century. These early Acts of Parliament forbade vagrancy and ordered beggars who could not maintain themselves, to remain in the parish where they were resident at the passing of the Act, or be sent back to the parish of their birth.

In 1601 an Act was passed which provided that the churchwardens and other substantial householders should be nominated each year as 'overseers of the poor'. It was the duty of the overseers to provide work for the poor, the cost of this to be funded by a poor rate, charged upon every inhabitant of the parish. This formed the basis of the Poor Law structure for the next 200 years.

Later in the 17th century Settlement Acts were introduced which restricted strangers settling in another parish, unless they rented property, or had sufficient funds to discharge the parish of any costs incurred on their behalf. Temporary workers or visitors had to carry a certificate from their own parish agreeing that they would be taken back.

Wragby workhouse was run by the church and was located in Louth Road opposite Silver Street. It was available as a public service for the poor of the village. Paupers, etc., who had no proper job to support themselves and/or their families, would be housed until they could obtain employment, which was usually on local farms. Even children as young as six or seven years old would do farm labouring such as picking potatoes, spreading manure and stone picking, as well as picking couch grass and twitch. Boys and girls under the age of 12 would earn around 4d (old Pence) to 1/- (one shilling) a day.

Local village doctors were appointed to look after the welfare of the inmates and if a pauper died in the workhouse burials were conducted as cheaply as possible. The fees allowed 1/6 each for the Vicar, Clerk and Sexton and 6d for tolling the bell.

Because the artificial protection of agriculture effectively ensured subsidised production of wheat, discouraged investment and the development of 'scientific' farming, it resulted in a downward spiral of depression. The situation steadily deteriorated, and with the prospect of employment in the expanding towns and cities, many people moved away from the land. In consequence many people became destitute and were forced into workhouses.

In 1830 the House of Lords held an investigation to determine the state of the country's poor and how they were treated. The Rev. Henry Foulis, Vicar of Wragby and Magistrate, was among many who were called upon to give testimony to them. The questions asked of him covered all aspects of life particularly Rent costs, Labour rates and if paid out of the Poor Rate or not and also whether men were employed in the winter months.

Regarding Wragby he stated: *'In my own Parish I am rather particularly circumstanced, for the whole of it belongs to a Cousin of mine, and the Poor's Rates do not amount to 3s. upon Two Thirds of the Rack Rent; and we give the poor, gardens and little accommodations. There are about 1,500 Acres, and the Population about 700'.* Asked if any part of the wages were paid out of the Poor Rate his reply was *'No; I have decidedly stopped it.'* He also revealed that the majority of men worked preparing clay in the winter months and earned 15s per week. The examiners also asked if there was a workhouse in the parish to which he replied that there was a *'small description of a workhouse'* which would hold 20 to 30 people but that no work was carried out in it as it was hardly ever used.

Thus in 1834 the Poor Law was introduced so that the Government effectively took over the problem of the poor and a new Workhouse was built in Horncastle to comply with this new arrangement. Wragby was now part of the Horncastle Union, which covered seven districts: Hemingby, Horncastle, Revesby, Tattershall, Tetford, Woodhall Spa and Wragby. The Workhouse in Wragby was subsequently closed and the residents transferred to Horncastle.

The last Governor of Wragby Workhouse was Mr. John Silvester. It is now the home of Bernard and Irene Andrews and also Hugh Bourn's drawing offices.

(The examination of Rev. Foulis took most of the day and only a small portion or it has been repeated here. For those of you who would like to know more you can access 'Appendix: poor laws: 14 December 1830', Journal of the House of Lords: volume 63: 1830-1831, pp. 540-48. at http://www.british-history.ac.uk/report.asp?compid=17015.)

The Forge

Situated on the Lincoln Road the Forge was in a prime position for passing trade as well as the locals. Records are too thin on the ground to establish exactly when the Forge started but according to the 1841 census, there were four Blacksmiths in Wragby at that time. Unfortunately this particular census does not give details of addresses but by judicial searching, we can establish that John Spencer was located on the Bardney Road. Leaving Charles Inman, Thomas Arden and John Smith unaccounted for. However, searching the Directories we find that William Arden was a Blacksmith in Wragby in 1792 followed in 1828 by Thomas Arden.

The Old Forge

It would appear that Thomas Arden died in Stamford in 1844 and that William Foster was listed as resident blacksmith on Lincoln Road in 1851. Charles Inman was pursuing his trade in Hagworthingham and of John Smith nothing has been found.

When William Foster left the Forge in 1876, at the age of 66, William Fanthorpe moved in with his wife and children. Much has been written about the Fanthorpe family elsewhere, so suffice it to say that he was well liked and took an active interest in local affairs. He left the Forge in 1902 and moved to Northamptonshire. At this time the Forge had been running for approximately 110 years and possibly longer.

It is believed the Forge ceased working around the time of World War II as the Cawdell family, who moved into the residence in the early 1950's, found plenty of anvils and horse shoes lying around.

The house still stands and is lived in to this day, as can be seen in the photograph below.

The Forge 2007
Note: A new two storey building has replaced part of the Forge

CLUBS OF OLD

Wragby Pig Club

The club was formed in 1844, seven years after Queen Victoria's accession to the throne in 1837. The Officers would meet at the Turner Arms Hotel quarterly in January, April, July and October.

The object of the club was to assist members when the loss of a pig or pigs took place and membership was restricted to residents of Wragby Parish. A notice about the club read as follows: "Any member losing a pig is entitled to receive the value of the animal, providing its value be under £8. There shall be an annual supper, held in the club room, on the first Thursday in December of each year. The supper to be on the tables at 7.00 p.m. at a charge of 1/6d for every member."

RULES.

1.—That this Society be denominated the Wragby Pig Club, and that the object of its members be to assist each other when the loss of a Pig or Pigs may take place. Each member must reside in Wragby.

2.—This Society shall have Two Trustees, a President, Treasurer, Secretary, and Six Committeemen, to be chosen every twelve months out of and by the members, who shall have the whole management of the affairs of the Club during the ensuing twelve months.

3.—The Officers shall meet at the "Turnors Arms" Hotel, in Wragby, on the second Saturday in January, April, July and October, from 8 to 9 p.m., when all contributions shall be paid.

4.—The President shall be paid the sum of Twelve Shillings and Sixpence, the Treasurer and Secretary the sum of Four Shillings and Sixpence each, for services rendered to the Society during their twelve months of office.

5.—That every person joining the Society shall pay two shillings and Sixpence to become a member, and Ninepence per quarter each for as many pigs as he may wish to enter, and Threepence per quarter towards Supper Fund, any member not paying his contributions on the first quarter night shall be fined Twopence, and the Secretary shall summon him to pay on the second quarter night all dues up to that time. Should he again neglect to pay, he will be deprived of all benefits.

6.—The amount of money to be kept in Treasurer's hands shall be Two Pounds; and all over and above that amount shall be placed in the Wragby Post Office Savings' Bank, in the names of the Treasurer and Trustees for the time being.

7.—Any Member losing a Pig, shall be entitled to receive from the Treasurer the value of the same, providing its value be under Eight Pounds, if the Fund be not sufficient to meet the demand the members shall immediately subscribe a sum in addition to their quarterly contributions to make up the deficiency.

8.—That Eight Pounds be the highest amount paid to a member for the loss of a Pig.

9.—There shall be a Yearly Meeting of the members, held in the Club Room, on the Second Saturday Night in January to choose a fresh Committee and Officers, and to Audit the Accounts.

10.—There shall be a Supper held in the Club Room, on the first Thursday in December of each year, the supper to be on the tables at 7 p.m., at a charge of One Shilling and Sixpence for every member present.

11.—Any Member swearing or behaving improperly, or wilfully offending another member at any meeting shall forfeit Sixpence to the Society.

12.—Any member purchasing more pigs than entered, shall give notice which pig or pigs he wishes to enter to the President, who shall wait upon the member, within three days, and if he decides that the pigs are healthy, they shall be duly marked and become club worthy, but pigs afterwards purchased shall not belong to the club until the former number is reduced.

13.—Any member not being in arrears, finding his pig diseased shall give notice to the President immediately, then two persons shall be appointed to value the same, the Officers to have the choice of one the owner the other. Should they not agree the two persons above shall appoint an unconcerned person whose decision shall be final.

14.—If any member owes more than two quarters contributions and his pig becomes diseased and should recover, it shall not be club worthy without the consent of the Committee for the time being.

15.—A Members Wife or Executor may still remain a member while living in the Parish of Wragby.

16.—That all monies belonging to this Society shall be paid to the Secretary.

17.—That any of the above Rules, may be altered by a majority at an Annual Meeting, and entered in the minute book kept for that purpose. Such alterations to be adhered to within seven days after the aforesaid meeting.

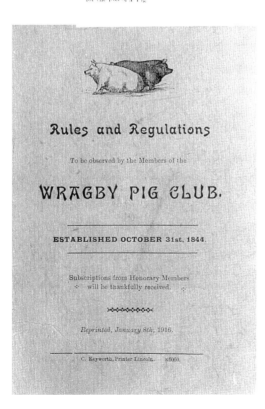

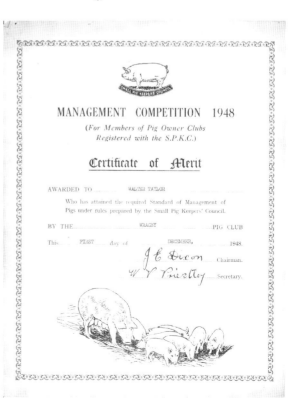

Sick and Dividing Club

Although information on the Club is very scarce, it is understood to have been formed in the 1920's. Members paid 1s to join and 6d per week. In 1965 the subscription was exactly the same. At that time Mr. C Whitehead was Chairman and sick members were paid 10s per week for eight weeks followed by 5s per week for six weeks. The maximum to be paid in any one year was £5 10s. Help was also given to any family where there was a bereavement.

An undated press release by a correspondent, Mr. J.E. Anderson read as follows:

"The annual share-out of the Wragby Sick and Dividing Club was held at the Turnor Arms Hotel last week, Mr. Clowes being in the Chair. The accounts for the past year showed £45 14s. 2d. paid out in sick pay, and, the dividend remaining for each of the 141 members was 19s. 4d. After the share-out the annual meeting was held when it was agreed to carry on the Club, the officers being re-elected as follows: Chairman, Mr. Clowes: secretary, Mr. P Priestley: treasurer, Mr. W. Rutland; with Messrs. W. Dunn, J. Dixon, S.Hill, C.Martin, and W. Picksley on the committee. A supper followed at which over 70 members were present. A vote of thanks was proposed to Mr. and Mrs. Clowes for the very excellent repast. The evening concluded with games and a sing song".

On a point of interest, Mr. W. Rutland was a founder member of the Club and still a member in 1965 when the Women's Institute Jubilee Year Book 1965 reported that "Clubs of this kind were slowly coming to an end, given the current conditions prevailing at that time".

Pelican Investment Club

According to a note left by Les Thorne this was started by Eric Dobson, Milkman roundsman, Councillor and Chairman of Housing, when the Old Peoples block was built on the Horncastle Road site.

Members met in the upper room of the Turnor Arms and paid £5 per month. The whole idea behind the Club was to learn something about investing, without risking a lot of money. Bankers and other financial experts, were invited to give talks to the membership.

The Club presumably started in 1962 as it is reported in the Women's Institute Jubilee Year Book 1965 that it was in its 3rd year. They had a limit of 50 members and a total of £50 invested each month. The Officials at that time were Chairman Mr G R Groome, Treasurer Mr R Potter, Secretary Mr. T Lockton, Asst. Secretary Mr. R Pask, Subscription Secretary Mr. A Shaw.

Unfortunately the Club was not too successful as, at the monthly meetings, tempers flared, and arguments arose as to what was, or was not the best investment. It was not long before all the shares were sold and the profits distributed to the members **not** to charity.

The name of the Club was taken from this well known Limerick by Dixon Lanier Meritt:

> What a wonderful bird is the Pelican,
> His bill holds more than his belican,
> He can take in his beak
> Enough food for a week
> But I'm damned if I see how the helican

SOCIAL CLUBS

Age Concern

During the Second World War, there were many additional difficulties for older people, which also revealed their existing problems. The result of a conference in 1940, was the formation of the Committee for the Welfare of the Aged.

Residents being entertained by the Brownies

The name Age Concern was adopted in 1970, and in 1973 Age Concern England was formed. Since then the national network has expanded rapidly, made up of independent local groups all working to improve the quality of life for older people.

After Newton Close was built in 1968, there were few organised activities for the residents of the sheltered housing. In 1973, Mrs. Ivy Cox approached Age Concern to see if they had any ideas. With the help and support of residents and Age Concern they held their first coffee morning, making just £15. A bank account was opened; Dr. Browne, the local doctor, was one of the signatories and Age Concern, Newton Close Group was 'in business'.

Parties, coffee mornings and trips became available to the residents, all approved by the resident warden, Mrs. Baldock. The local Royal Antediluvian Order of Buffaloes kindly donated a wheelchair, which was the start of a very healthy collection of aids. Over the years Age Concern has helped many people by providing aids such as commodes, walkers, zimmers and wheel-chairs; all on short term loans but very necessary when the need arises.

At the time of writing in 2007, Age Concern continues to thrive and Mrs. Boyd, the sister of Mrs. Cox, is still actively involved after more than 34 years. Clearly over the past 34 years many others have contributed to the success of the Group and readers will remember Dr. & Mrs. Browne, Jim Baldock, Jack Cole, Pastor Jack Brown, Charlie Ward, June Wordle, Elsie Crow and Yvonne Blackburn, the present Secretary, who has held the post since 1981.

The Group meets weekly and have quite a hectic social life and 'Outsiders' are now most welcome and encouraged to attend the gatherings, so that the sometimes forgotten age group are always remembered on Newton Close

Disability Lincs

The Group started in the mid 1970's as the Lincolnshire Society for the Physically Handicapped. Disabled people were referred by Social Services and a qualified occupational therapist took charge of the weekly, regional craft classes. The Wragby class belonged to the Horncastle Committee until 1977, when it became a separate branch with its own committee. Formerly, annual county rallies were held at many places, including Cranwell and Grimsthorpe Castle, where all branches would be entertained.

Members and Volunteers of Disability Lincs holding garments made for Romanian Aid
Back Row L-R: Janet Kiddle, Janet Lenton, Anne Flint, Sarah Bellhouse
Seated: Betty Whitely, Olive Paul, R.O.A.D. Representative-Paul Elliott, Susan Robinson

Over the years Wragby has raised funds to finance monthly outings in summer, meals in winter and various projects to help the disabled members. In 1988 the branch lost its occupational therapist, the committee ran the classes until 1995 when Margaret Sutherland was officially appointed.

The name of the Society was changed in 1993 to 'Disability Lincs', the name was chosen from suggestions sent in by branches. This was Wragby's suggestion!

Disability Lincs not only raises funds for outings. It was decided that it would be of great benefit, for the disabled members, if a hoist could be installed at the Wragby Swimming Pool. Over £2000 was needed, so a whole series of events were planned; a big barbeque, coffee mornings, raffles and auctions amongst the members; in other words almost anything to boost the fund. The group were very pleased with the support it received from the people of Wragby, the target was reached, and the hoist installed.

Members holding their Certificates for using the new Hoist at the Swimming Pool
Back L-R: Pam Chapman, Monica Bourn, Olive Paul, Margaret Sutherland
Front L-R: Phyliss Frankish, Margaret Clark

The Group has recently suffered from cuts in Social Services funding. Jessica Foster and Sarah Bellhouse are now running the classes on a voluntary basis so that they can continue.   Just as it has for over 30 years, the club meets weekly at the Town Hall on Tuesday morning. The outings and meals at the Town Hall, prepared by local volunteers, are still enjoyed by all. It goes without saying that Disability Lincs are always looking for new volunteers with fresh ideas and energies to help with their activities.

Mothers Union

As many people are not fully aware of this group we have given a brief history of its beginnings.

Mary Sumner founded the Society in 1876 for the support of women in their role as mothers. Almost 20 years later a Control Council was formed, unifying members across diocese into a National Union. Queen Victoria was the Patron and Mary Sumner the first President. By 1900 the Mothers Union had 170,000 members with branches overseas.

Today the Mothers Union's range and depth of work far exceeds Mary Sumner's original vision of a circle of prayer upholding family life with 3.6 million members in 78 countries.

It is not entirely clear when the All Saint's, Wragby Branch of the Mothers Union started in Wragby but insofar as some of the older residents can recall it must be at least 50-60 years ago.   Flo Shepherd still has her membership card dated 1954.

Meetings were held, monthly, in the Church. They started with a short service, followed by a speaker and then they went for tea, in the Town Hall. Coffee mornings were held regularly and one raised £90 towards a new carpet for the Church.

Mothers Union Coffee Morning

In 1965 the officers were: Mrs. N. Lancaster-Enrolling Member; Mrs. F. Seely-Secretary; Mrs. R. Bones-Treasurer with Mrs. M. Dunn, the Diocesan representative.

Since then the meetings have been held variously in the Church, the Vicarage, the Methodist Church and members' homes. The format has changed little from a short service, an invited speaker, the serving of refreshments and now, outings or other interesting topics.

The Branch continues to meet regularly every month, usually at 2 p.m. on the first Monday, with the guidance of appointed officials. Venues vary, now often in the homes of members, still in the usual format with the recent addition of a Christmas lunch.

Scout & Guide Association

It is a century or thereabouts since Scouts (1907) and Guides (1910) were formed by Robert Baden-Powell and his sister Agnes. The overall aim of the Association was to bring out in each individual his/her unique talents and abilities and develop them to the full, and this has little changed over the years.

The Scout Group was formed in Wragby in 1943, whilst the Brownie Unit, which was closed during the War (no earlier details can be found), re-started in January 1973 by Mrs. Sowden with the help of Nora Shaw; Brenda Bodily started to help Nora in 1979. At this time the Guide's met in Wragby Youth Centre under the name of 1st Barkwith pack. This continued until 1992, when a new name was registered as the 1st Wragby Guide Unit. The Rainbow Unit was opened in 1988, when Andrea Ward decided there was a need for something for the younger girls. Over the years the various Units of the Wragby Association have met in the Wragby Youth Centre and Wragby Primary School.

A community project, in every sense of the word, started in 1989, when it was determined the Wragby Group needed premises of their own. A public meeting was called in August and it was decided to form a Committee entitled "Wragby Uniformed Joint Headquarters Management Committee" with Gordon Fiddler as Chairman/Treasurer and Andrea Ward, Rainbow and Ranger Guider, as Secretary. The other Committee members were, Mr. Russ Millson - Group Scout Leader; Graham Turner - Scout Leader;

Sandra Turner - Akala Cub Leader; Mo Fricke - Beaver Leader; Chris Marflitt - Assistant Beaver Leader; Anne Buffham and Audrey South - Assistant Rainbow Guiders; Brenda Bodily - Brown Owl of Brownies; Alice Hodgson - Girl Guide Leader.

Mrs. Linda Bell, Mrs. Karen Bruntlett, Mrs. Kathy Lowe and Mrs. Audrey South, who were the fundraising committee, did an amazing job of organising so many events, almost on a weekly basis, to make sure the finances were raised for the project. Events included disco's, jumble sales, stalls at Wragby Show and the Christmas Market, cheese and wine evenings, fun runs, sherry and mince pie mornings, carol singing, clothes parties, gang shows, a Christmas Show, roller skating every Saturday and a mammoth tombola. By the summer of 1990 over £5000 had been raised. Although the giant tombola raised the most money, for an event, it didn't quite make the Guinness book of records, as they had hoped. The funds had been helped with a single donation of £1139 from the Liberal 100 Club, and varying amounts from other organisations who wished to be associated with the project.

The meetings, of the Committee, were held at the home of Mr. & Mrs. Fiddler to save money. They, fortunately, had a timber building donated by Mr. Steve Allcock, and several willing dads helped Mr. John Bell to dismantle the building and store it at Holton Power Farmers. The Scout Leader, Graham Turner, successfully approached the Wragby Parish Council with a view to leasing a plot of land at the junction of Wire Hill Lane and Louth Road, and planning consent was sought.

As the money rolled in plans went ahead and in view of the Committee's inexperience at overseeing the project, Mr. John Pearson kindly agreed to act as foreman. Local businesses were used throughout and volunteers from the community also came to help. After two years, a total of £10,500 had been raised. The Grand Opening took place in May 1991 and, because of John Pearson's hard work, it was agreed to name the building "Pearson Lodge".

The Opening of Pearson Lodge
L-R: Graham Turner, Sandra Turner, Audrey South, Ann Buffham, Andrea Ward
Mo Fricke, Brenda Bodily, Chris Marflitt, Martin Holcombe, Gordon Fidler

Some years after the opening of Pearson Lodge planning permission was granted for a portacabin to be situated on the site to be used as storage for equipment. The viability of the Wragby Units continues to be dependent on volunteers giving up their time to train and run them, and, of course, the availability of interested boys and girls, all with the full support of a Management Committee.

For one reason or another there had not been any Beaver, Cub or Scout Units for some time. However, Sandra Turner(Cub Scout Leader) has recently returned to the ' fold ' supported by David Kitchen who is in training as a Scout Leader. Brenda Bodily and Andrea Ward are still with the Brownies and Rainbows, respectively and Jenny Bolton is the current Guide Leader.

A weekly subscription is levied on every boy and girl, part of which goes to the Headquarters Management Committee in support of expenditure on the maintenance and services of the H/Q building, including insurance and emergency telephone. Fundraising is still ongoing with the main event being the Wragby Christmas Market and Grand Raffle.

Women's Institute (W.I.)

On 12th January 1944, a few ladies met to discuss the possibility of forming an Institute. At the meeting, in the Methodist Schoolroom, they were addressed by Mrs. Winifred Hall, the National Secretary of the movement. The result of the meeting was that 25 ladies entered their names for membership and another five apologised for not being able to attend. The formal motion proposing the formation was moved by Mrs. R. Skipworth and seconded by Mrs. R. Bygott.

The first organised meeting was held in the old Grammar School. Mrs. S. Bradshaw was elected the first President, Mrs. F. Thorne – Vice President, Mrs. J. Anderson – Secretary and Mrs. Bygott – Treasurer. As this was a time of 'make do and mend' the newly formed group made gloves and slippers, the slippers being made from old felt hats. By November 1944 they had joined forces with the Young Farmers Club in buying a piano and on one memorable night in the old Grammar School, they did the Lancers ! Anyone who knows the school would realise what a squeeze this must have been, but we are assured they did manage to get in the middle of the floor.

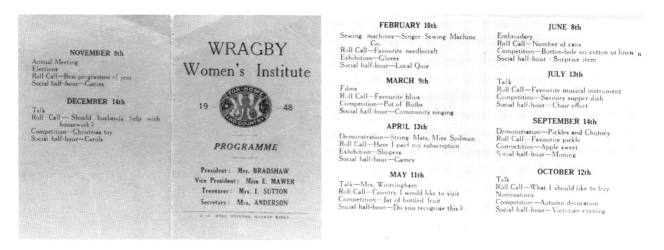

The first Produce Show, run with the help of the Young Farmers, had 200 entries and raised £14. Their 12 strong choir sang in Lincoln Cathedral and many amusing events were held to lighten the memories of the war. In 1947 they put on a play entitled *'World Without Men'* which was seen by 77 members. This was only the forerunner of many plays/sketches which have been performed since.

Notoriety hit in 1950 when the local and National Press got hold of reports that some of the Committee had run off with funds and something about a trip to 'Torrington Docks', and they wanted to know what it was all about. It turned out that Wragby WI had been holding a 'mock' meeting, in which a fictitious balance sheet and a trip were discussed, obviously someone had got the wrong end of the stick.

This 1950 notoriety was history, when a new image of Wragby WI made the local and National Sunday newspapers. A mistake in a news-sheet left members in a state of feverish anticipation when the news-sheet asked them to 'name their favourite lover'. No wonder the next meeting was packed, when the president Margaret Kane explained it was a printer's slip and should have read 'name your favourite flower'. It was reported that instead of telling tales of seduction they rallied round to help the disadvantaged, preparing shoe boxes of aid for Bosnia.

In 1965, the 60 years Jubilee of the County WI coincided with the 21st birthday of Wragby WI, which not only celebrated in style with a party but also compiled the *W.I. Jubilee Year Book 1965*. This book has proved a valuable source of information, for current research. Mrs. L. Potter chaired the birthday and the honoured guests were three past Presidents; Mrs. S. J. Bradshaw, Mrs. Rex Cooper and Mrs. H. Shuttleworth. Mrs. A. Philips, another former President, had unfortunately, died. Mrs. R. Bones had been chosen to attend the Royal Garden Party, at Buckingham Palace. It was reported she was introduced to the Duchess of Gloucester who admitted that she had not heard of a place called Wragby.

Members of the W.I. Celebrating their 21st Anniversary

WI is still going strong, meeting every month in the Town Hall. They organise many items and outings of interest and always have a guest speakers at their meetings. They also offer help in the community and do a fantastic job of catering at the annual Wragby Show and Country Fayre. The current President is Margaret Kane.

Youth Club & Sports Centre

The earliest form of Youth Club, in Wragby, started during World War II when two gangs of lads, one run by Malcolm Applewhite and the other run by Ron Brothwell, were taken in hand by Sergeant Busty Rawlins, of the Royal Engineers, who were stationed in Wragby for a while. He made them wooden rifles and eventually formed an Army Cadet Force with meetings being held in the Bowls Pavilion at the Turnor Arms. After the war ended this was disbanded.

A new Youth Club was also held in the school room of the Methodist Church run by Henry Parkin, about 1955-56. Around the same time a local policeman, PC Ted Farrow, started a club in the little room at the Turnor Arms, assisted by Doug Clarke and Joyce Ward.

In 1957 a Youth Club was held in the Chalet, led by Peter Nunn. The Committee, on 15th February 1957 was Colin Skipworth - Chairman, Jean Clarke - Secretary, Judy Stephenson - Assistant Secretary, Joyce Ward - Treasurer. Rex Keal and Doug Clarke were also on the committee.

In the early 1960's, a Youth Club was started by PC Ted Farrow, in an old Nissan hut in Reg Halls yard which was situated on the Horncastle Road. He was assisted by John Harris and later joined by Brian Melton and Mick Shepherd.

On 14th December 1965 a new timber and brick constructed Youth Club was built in Silver Street, where the Pre-School building now stands. It was partly built by Holmes Joinery, internally finished by Youth members and organised by John Harris and Brian Melton.

When the Primary School moved to Silver Street in 1968, the old buildings were converted into a Youth Centre. It opened on 14th October 1970. Later, new squash courts were built in the old school playground and they opened on 1st December 1978.

After the Youth Centre was completed, a massive fund raising campaign was launched to build a Sports Hall. This campaign was headed by a Management Committee and chaired by Paul Johnson. Youth Club members and adults alike worked tirelessly to achieve this aim. Grant aid was received from The Sports Council, Lincolnshire County Council, East Lindsey District Council as well as Wragby Parish Council. The Sports Hall opened on 8th January 1990.

In recent times Michael Shepherd, Kevin Createaux and Lynda Hillreiner have served as Leaders-in-Charge supported by Dennis Blackburn, Pam Till, Liz Andrew, Pete Hutchinson, Rachel Horn, Christine Williams, Pete Hillreiner, Anthony Jervis and Roger Height.

Wragby Youth Club Hut - 1965 at the corner of the School Playing Field

Youth Club by B. Steel - 19th June 1964

The new youth club at the Town Hall has nearly been built. They have to put the roof on and there is still a lot to do inside. Last Monday night when I went to bed I tripped on a mat and my tooth came out.

Sports

Bowls Club

The earliest bowls club in Wragby probably started around 1920 and played on a site between the Adam & Eve and the old grammar school. Subsequently the Turnor Arms had a bowling green. This was used from the late 1930's to the early 1950's which was on the site of the present car park.

Bowling Club Members 1936

**Back Row L-R: Mr. C. Whitely, Mr. Billy Mawer, Mr. Jim Pollard, Mr. Herbert,
Mr. A. Mumby (Headmaster), Mr. Rowsen, Mr. Jack Albones
Front Row L-R: Mr. Doughty, Mr. Chambers, Mr. Twidale, Mr. Ernest Whiteley,
Mr. G.C. Musson, Mr. Bratley**

The present club, Dove Park Bowls Club, was formed in 1971 at a meeting held in Wragby Town Hall. George Woolgar, the local newsagent and good friend of the club, observed that the club had no money, and donated £20 to start the club on its way. The committee was comprised of members from other clubs.

The green was prepared on land previously used by Mr. Denis Bartholomew for chicken and egg production. After Mr. Bartholomew retired, Mr. A. B. Dove, JP, presented the field to the Parish of Wragby for recreational purposes. It was decided to name the new club after Mr. Dove, a move which gave him great pleasure.

The area to be used for bowling needed some trees, which were an obstruction, to be removed, drains installed and the site levelled This work was carried out by Rowan Crymble, a local farmer, who was also a qualified civil engineer, assisted by other club members. On completion, the new green was left to settle for a year.

Mr. Dove opened Dove Park bowling green, in June 1974, by bowling the first wood down the green watched by some of the officials of the bowls club. Among the guests at the opening was Mr. Peter Tapsell,

MP. During the opening year, limited games were played on what is now a popular green in the shadow of All Saint's Church. Present membership stands at around 30 who play in three different leagues.

Football

The earliest record of the Football Club is the photograph of the team in 1907 but whether there was a team before that is not known. The Club has continued to have a football team for nearly every season since 1907, either adult, children or both.

Football Team 1907

The Club has always played in a black and white striped football kit and has played on various local grounds but mainly the ground has been based on the Lincoln Road site. Wragby owes a lot to Mr. Shuttleworth for the use of his field and allowing the Club to continue to use it, because without it there would be no Club.

Wragby Football Club entered the village trophy in 1919, for the first time. Since then they have had seven appearances in the semi-finals. They were also Champions of the North Lincoln Village Football League in the 1922-23 season. They won the village trophy in the 1982-83 season with Benny Hinchcliffe as the manager. Clearly there have been many managers over the past 100 years and names such as Bratton, Ward, King, Hutchinson, Blackburn, Wright, Reeson, Lomas, Lowman and Waters are familiar to many.

More recently Wragby has 4 teams: Men's, Under 10's, Under 12's and Under 13's, allowing some 51 people to play football on a Sunday.

Like many village organisations, the Club has to be self-funding, with voluntary support of the community and this comes down to a dedicated, strong committee. One such example is the 1946 Contrasts Revue with all proceeds going to the Wragby Football Club.

WRAGBY FOOTBALL CLUB.
Season 1922-23.

President : Dr. G. DEANE, Wragby.

Vice-Presidents :

C. LANGHAM, Esq., Panton ; R. BYGOTT, Esq., "Beech House," Wragby ;
and T. E. FREARSON, Esq., "Barkwith House," Wragby.

Chairman : W. JOHNSON.

Captain : I. SUTTON.   Vice-Captain : W. BROTHWELL.

Hon. Treasurer : A. MAWER.   Hon. Secretary : J. W. ANDERSON.

Selection Committee : E. WHITLEY, W. ALLIS, G. BROTHWELL,
C. ELLERKER and W. E. RUTLAND.

OFFICIAL PROGRAMME   -   Price 2d.

We extend a hearty welcome to all visitors here to-day, and hope they will enjoy the outing and go away with pleasant recollections of their Trip to Wragby.

Our League Record is as follows : Played 16, Won 14, Drawn 0, Lost 2, Goals for 87, and Goals against 10.

The two Matches we lost were both by the odd goal in three, and away from home, against Market Rasen and Nettleham.

We do not wish to blow our trumpets further, but naturally feel proud of such a record.

We attribute our success to the following reasons :— We have been able to place the same eleven in the field for the majority of the matches, in fact, during the whole of the season we have only called upon two reserves. To the hard work done by our energetic Secretary, J. W. Anderson. The good feeling and comradeship that has always existed amongst the players. The interest that is shewn in the Club by all in Wragby and District, and the willing help and support we always receive from them.

North Lincoln Village Football League
SEASON 1922-23.

Wragby (Champions) v. Rest of League,
Beech House Ground, Wragby,

On SATURDAY, APRIL 21st, 1923,

Kick-off 3 p.m. sharp.   Collection on Ground.

Right.   WRAGBY.   Left.

Black and White Stripes.

*J. Jessop.

H. Shuttleworth.   *W. Brothwell

*Joe Brothwell.   *I. Sutton (Capt.)   G. Sayer.

*A. Mawer.   *F. Seely.   G. Smith.   A. Hebb.   L. Shuttleworth.

Referee :—   Linesmen :—

J. E. LONGDEN,   W. LILLIE, Dunholme.

Langworth.   — LYON, Welton.

Drury   A. Jubb   H. Priestley   Atkinson   S. Margrave.
(Welton). (Nettleham).   (Holton)   (Nettleham). (Fillingham).

Lillie   Pindar   Richardson
(Dunholme).   (Bishop Norton)   (Langworth).

S. Parkin (Capt., Welton).   Parker (M. Rasen)

Bennett (Bishop Norton)

Left.   REST OF LEAGUE.   Right.

* Denotes previous Cup Winners.

PUBLIC TEA in the Schoolroom at 5 p.m., 1/- each.

The CUP and MEDALS will be presented in the Schoolroom at 6 p.m., by Mr. S. T. Robinson, Dunholme, League President.

SMOKING CONCERT, Turner Arms Hotel, at 8 p.m.

W. J. Harrison, General Printer, High Bridge, Lincoln.

WRAGBY FOOTBALL CLUB

Saturday, December 21st,
1946

'CONTRASTS'
The New
Black & White Revue
Presented in
The CHALET, WRAGBY

Souvenir Programme
Price 3d.

CREDITS

The Wragby Football Club wish to record their
thanks to the following for their generosity :—

Mr. WATTAM—Loan of Chalet.
Mr. G. HOLMES—Amplifying Equipment.
Mr. LOWMAN—Lighting Effects,
and all others who so kindly assisted.

The Dresses were designed and executed by
Mrs. HAYWARD

Original Sketches and Production by
STAN A. HAYWARD

All Proceeds to the
WRAGBY FOOTBALL CLUB

PROGRAMME

1	Intro.	"Theme" (Tchaikovsky) ....
		"Lily Marlene" ....
		Compere—Betty Piano—John
		Violin—Albert Solo—Taffy
		" Black and White" Chorus
2	Sketch	"Love Finds a Way" ....
		Pat, Trot, Myrtle, Leslie,
		Edward and Stan
3	Scena	"Song of the Islands" ....
		Dorothy and Margaret
		Pat, Peggy and Margaret
4	Silhouette	"The Operation" ....
		Betty, Joan and Stan
5	Latest Hits	"Down in the Valley" ....
		"Bless You" ....
		"Let him go, let him tarry" ....
		Piano—Mrs. Wilkinson Solo—Stan
		" Black and White" Chorus

6	Sketch	"School Days" ....
		Edward, Pat, Peggy,
		Dorothy, John and Charles
7	Quiz	Cash or Forfeit ....
		Quizmaster—Charles
8	Sketch	"Down on the Farm" ....
		Edmund, Binky, Molly,
		Mrs. Dove, Leslie and Edward
9	Finale	"Tribute to Britain" ....
		Piano—Mrs. W. Violin—Albert
		Soloists—Mrs. Paul and Taffy
		" Black and White" Chorus
		Molly, Dorothy and Margaret
		"Goodnight" ....
		Betty and Entire Company

GOD SAVE THE KING

Football Team c.1912

Over the years with support from the local farmers, builders and parents, the Club has been able to continue and be where it is today. Recent help from the Parish Council has enabled the Club to make vast improvement to the ground, and the grass cutting services provided are of great help to the Club.

Of course, it must be said that funding has not always been one-way. The Club also generates money for deserving causes such as St Barnabas Hospice, Everyman and Hospitals, by way of charity football matches, race nights and even men's waxing!

Under 12's Football Team 1990's

Rifle Club

The Club was founded in 1900 and by 1922 claimed to be the oldest Club in the County. As you will have read in Herbert Banks profile, he was considered a crack shot. Therefore, it will come as no surprise that, at one time, he was Match Secretary and responsible for training many marksmen who made good in the First World War.

In 1913 Thomas Henry Ranyard was the Honorary Secretary of the Club and, from the 1913 postal competition score sheet below, clearly Wragby Rifle Club was on a winning streak. On closer scrutiny it seems both the Match and Honorary Secretaries were slightly off form on that day in May against Caistor.

L.C.M.R.A.
Postal Competition,   1913.
DIVISION... *I* ....

NAME OF CLUB......... *Wragby* ....

VERSUS...... .... *Caistor*

WEEK ENDING............ *May 31st*

NAME.	FOR USE OF SCRUTINEERS.
T. Rodwell	98
W. Harrison	98
G. Cottingham	97
G. Rowson	97
F. Thorne	96
G. Smith	94
H. J. Banks	92
G. Ranyard	90
G. Hebb	90
E. Whitley	87
Total	762
Opponent	739
HIGHEST SCORE OF MATCH — T. Rodwell : W. Harrison	98

(Signed) *George Blunett*   Scrutineer

The results sheet for a postal competition

By 1922 the Club had twice attained second place in the league; beyond that it is not known when the Club finally folded.

Whether or not Herbert Banks shooting talent was passed on in his genes is not known but, as can be seen in the photograph, one of his four daughters was certainly following in his footsteps.

**Mr. Banks' daughter
shooting at Wragby School c.1912**

In a letter dated April 9th 1934 from Don Oswin, Honorary Secretary of the Lincoln Constitutional Rifle Club addressed to a *"Dear Sir"* (whoever that was) refers to them having *'The Year of the Rifle Club'* photo taken. *"As you are one of the Vice Presidents we wondered if you would accept one with the Club's best wishes hoping you are better from your accident".* It is known that Herbert Banks had a serious accident in 1933 and subsequently died on 7th September 1934. Could the 'Dear Sir' referred to have been Herbert Banks?

Cycling

Although at the present time nothing is known about the cycling club in Wragby, it is apparent from the photograph below, that it must have been a flourishing group of enthusiasts.

Wragby Men's Cycling Club 1907

Swimming

The first swimming pool in Wragby is thought to have been the one created by Headmaster Mr. Herbert J. Banks. In 1898 he experimented with a temporary dam in the beck and a year later built the first village swimming pool in England. The pupils of the school and other volunteers helped him to do this in the

Swimming Club c.1901

evenings. A permanent dam was erected to raise the level of the water to a sufficient depth and the pool excavated to increase the width from 8 feet to 24 feet and to a length of 45 yards. The sides of the pool were later lined with old sleepers. Additionally a wooden shed, comprising two rooms, was built on the bank. Not only was swimming taught in the pool but also life saving techniques for which certificates were awarded, usually presented by Lady Mary Turnor. Annual competitions and displays by Lincoln's finest swimmers were an annual event, which drew huge crowds.

The Swimming Pool in the late 1930's
(Only the swimsuits change)

WRAGBY

Swimming Club

(Member's Card)

SEASON 193♥. ↳

President:
Mr. H. J. Banks.

Secretary:
R. W. P. Picksley.

Chairman:
W. Taylor.

Treasurer:
A. Taylor.

Committee:
J. W. Anderson. J. G. B. Holmes.
W. Dixon. W. Berry. C. Berry
and G. Dales.

> *Any person throwing or pushing children into the Swimming Pool will be immediately expelled from the Club.*

In the late 1920's the pool was organised by Arthur Taylor. When a child could swim across the pool, they were awarded with a certificate and a shilling.

In May 1972, a special meeting was called to discuss a swimming pool project for the primary school. The PTA. at the time, had £178 and certain pledges, which brought the total to £578. After a lot of research and discussion, it was decided that a cheap, quick scheme would not be at all satisfactory and so a more permanent type of pool was sought.

Swimming Pool under construction 1973

The first phase was completed and opened on 1st September 1973 at a cost of £2500. All the extra funds were raised from donations and special events. The next phase, to provide nearly all year round cover, was completed in May 1974 and was handed over to the Education Authority by the PTA. in June of that year. Many people turned out to look round the pool and have tea with the staff and parents. The total cost was nearly £4000, of which £3750 had been raised locally.

In November that same year, at their Annual General Meeting, the PTA. declared that all outstanding pool bills had been paid and gave thanks to all who had helped along the way. Both children and adults were using the pool to learn how to swim and it was a definite asset to the community

The present indoor swimming pool was built in 1997/98 again through the generosity of the community and sponsors. It is run by a management committee and is open every day and most evenings. The pool is now of a more permanent nature and is open all year round. It caters not only for the able bodied but also the disabled, having a chair lift to facilitate entering and leaving the pool. Maintenance and fuel costs run high and the Pool Committee run monthly Quiz Nights, occasional Boot Fairs, an Alphabet Quiz and Evenings of Entertainment to raise the necessary funds.

Swimming Pool Building 2007

Tennis

That there was a thriving tennis club in the village can be seen from the following photograph, taken towards the end of the 19th century, Unfortunately no further records can be found.

Wragby Tennis Club c.1898

Cricket

Wragby once fielded a cricket team but for how long, is not known. The Wragby Cricket Club was formed by Mr. Priestley (middle row, right) and Mr. Bygott (middle row, left). The photograph belongs to Mrs. E. Denton, daughter of Mr. Priestley, who still has her father's bat and ball.

Wragby Cricket Club Team 1924

Hockey

Not much is known about the Wragby & District Hockey Team, when it started or when it disbanded. The photograph below is all we have. The ladies in the picture are: N. Whitley, M. Smith, G. Doughty, P. Dales, I. Denny, J. Greenfield, E. Frow, T. Weightman, Mrs. Horton, R. Heath and M. Osbourne.

Ladies Hockey Team 1937/8

Badminton Club

About the same time as the Town Hall was being built, it was Mr. Bones and Mr. Cartwright who were the instigators in requesting the Hall be big enough for a badminton court – they were clearly listened to as the court is there to this day. At present Badminton can be played at both the Town Hall and the Sports Hall. The photograph, taken in 1959 by Mr. Bones, shows some of the enthusiasts who were there on that December day.

Gents L-R: Peter Shepherd, Percy Cartwright, Bill Broadhead, Alan Coxhead, Clive Dewhurst
Ladies L-R: Mary Lee, Judy Snowdon, Margaret Seely, Norma Robinson, Sheila Dewhurst

Keep Fit

To do most sports you have to be fit and healthy, so what better way to end this section than with a picture of the Wragby Ladies Keep Fit Club of the early 1960's.

Wragby Ladies Keep Fit Club
Back: Mrs. R. Hall, Mrs. F. Hillreiner, Mrs. A. Harris, Mrs. J. Humberstone,
Mrs. M. Hoyes, Mrs. M. Wright, A. Bush, P. Paul, Mrs. U. Woolgar
Front: Mrs. J. Shepherd, B. Allen, S. Woolgar, Mrs. N. Shaw

MISCELLANY

A Two Headed Baby

Wragby became the centre of attention in 1676 when it was announced that the wife of one Charles Gays gave birth to a male child with two heads. The child lived for some hours and it was stated that the mother had kept an Inn in the town. Although an incredible story it was apparently given much credence throughout the area.

Wilkinsons

Situated on the Horncastle Road, next to Turner Square and opposite the Adam & Eve, used to stand Wragby's Toll Booth. Being one of the first in the Country it was of major importance but ceased collecting toll charges in the late 1800's.

In the 1930's Ernest Whitley ran a small greengrocery business there. He had a small counter and shelving to display produce but, with three people in the shop it was bursting at the seams. This must surely have been in the running for the country's smallest shop! Mr. Whitley also sold men's working boots which were displayed on wooden stands outside in fine weather.

Mr. Whitley retired in 1945 and Arthur and Phyllis Wilkinson carried on the business adding tinned food sales. While Mrs. Wilkinson was busy in the shop, Mr. Wilkinson was towing a small truck behind his bicycle selling produce around Wragby and the neighbouring villages. He later bought a small van allowing him greater freedom of choice, in his produce range, and speedy deliveries to customers.

In the 1950's local school children could buy broken bags of crisps for a penny and also penny bars of chocolate - real bargains!

**Olive Dixon crossing school children from Wilkinson's
to the Adam & Eve c.1960**

Mr. & Mrs. Wilkinson retired in 1966 and the building was knocked down in the 1970's after a lorry crashed into the shop making the foundations and building unsafe. Today it would probably have been the subject of a preservation order.

An Old Fashioned Will

In 1535 one Thomas Heven, Gentleman of Wragby, in his will, left to his wife *"one sylver goblet and six sylver sponys not gylted, and one sylver salte parcell bylte with a cover, and 20 marks. A priest is to sing for my soule, Jane my my wyff's soule, Anne my wyff's welfare, my fader and moder's soules."* (Lincolnshire Wills 1500-1600 - Cannon Maddison F.S.H.)

Weather gives Wragby a Whirl

The normal peace of a Sunday evening, in Wragby, was shattered by a freak whirlwind. Lasting barely five minutes, the storm caused a lot of damage and in one instance picked up a 15 cwt muck spreader, carrying it over a chicken shed and depositing it in a field 100 yards away. The machine, belonging to Mr. Joe Jessup of Goltho, was totally wrecked and the roof of his corn store was ripped off.

Mr. & Mrs. Musson returned to their home, in the Market Place, at 6.30 pm and noticed that the roofs of all three outbuildings had gone. The timber supports, as well as the tiles, had been swept away. Mr. Musson was relieved however, to find that his pigs were still alive and well in one of the buildings. Mrs. Johnson, opposite, had watched the roofs go, along with the globes off their petrol pumps.

Mr. Merryweather, a farm worker who had been working on the Market Rasen side of Wragby, had a narrow escape when a flying tile crash landed nearby.

Red Kites

The last breeding pair of Red Kites was seen in Wragby in 1870, which was also the last recorded stronghold in Lincolnshire. Nothing has been recorded since apart from one or two occasions in the 1970's when sightings were recorded flying over the Wash. Until, that is, one was found dead, in 1988, on a farm in Kirton Lindsay some 20 miles from Wragby. Experts believe that Mr. Terry Bradshaw, who found the bird, was the first person in this area to handle a bird of this type in 118 years. It was thought the bird had died of a broken neck and may have flown over from Scandinavia.

The Red Kite was taken to Scunthorpe museum where it was on display, once it had been stuffed.

"Red Kite, found near Kirton in Lindsey, now on display at North Lincolnshire Museum."

"Reproduced by kind permission of North Lincolnshire Council."

Home for Tea

During the Lincolnshire Uprising of 1536, Wragby sent 200 of her men to join the march from Horncastle to Lincoln. Apparently they arrived about teatime and were told to go home again, which they did!

Treasure Trove

In January 1980 Mr. B. Houlden, of The Crescent, was digging in his back garden for worms to use as bait, when to his amazement he found buried treasure! He had unearthed three rings: one gold and two silver, which were declared Treasure Trove by H.M. Coroner for Lincoln the following month. The rings were subsequently acquired by the County Council Museum and are described below. Their present location is unknown.

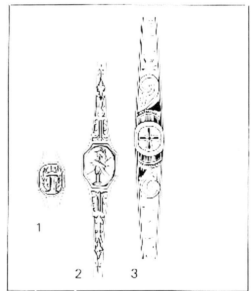

Plate VII   Gold and silver rings from Wragby   British Museum

1.   Pure gold Sygnet Ring with sub-rectangular bezel engraved with the letter I, a crown above and two debased fronds of foliage on either side. Thought to date around the late 15th - early 16th Century.

2.   Silver ring with octagonal bezel set with an oval Cornelian carved with a bird with the head of Minerva in a Corinthian helmet. The shoulders of the square sectioned hoop have a symmetrical scroll decoration left in reserve against a keyed ground which would have been filled with niello or enamel. Thought to date around the mid 16th Century.

3.   Silver ring with a circular bezel with four pointed ovals arranged in a cross. The shoulders are decorated with scrolls. Thought to date around the late 15th - early 16th Century.

Tokens also found in the area of Wragby

Ice Cream

Where E.H. Thorne's offices now stand, there used to be a pair of small cottage. In the early to mid 1920's, one of them was occupied by Mr. Taylor. During the summer months Mr. Taylor used to make ice cream, which he carried around in the basket of a baker's delivery bicycle. The ice cream was packed in blocks of ice and he had an unusual call sign, for children. He would say *"What do you do when your mother hits you?"* Back came the reply - *"I scream!"* You can imagine how that would go down in today's atmosphere of political correctness!

Fish and Chips

It appears that there has been a fish and chip shop in Wragby since the 1920's. It was run by Mr. Barter in 1930, who was a member of the Holmes family. The fish was cut into size ready for frying, the potatoes peeled and cut into chips, all by hand. A very tedious job indeed.

Mr. And Mrs. Farmery came to Wragby in 1930, living first in Bardney Road they later moved into the house behind the café and sweet shop. They took over the chippy during the war and their daughter Gladys ran the café. When Mr. Farmery died in 1947, his daughter, now Mrs. Taylor, took over the running of the fish and chip shop with her husband. It wasn't until the shop was sold to Mr. Drake in the 1950's that it was moved to its present location, where the café and sweet shop used to be.

Fish and Chips were also sold from the Turnor Arms, by landlady, Mrs. Dolly Clowes, from 1954 to 1956 - but only on Fridays and Saturdays. Mr. & Mrs. A. Paul also had a fish shop in a tin hut at the rear of what is now Market Place Stores.

Looking at the photograph below, the fish and chip shop used to be where the laundette is and the café and sweet shop was where the fish café is shown. Next door to the café there was a butcher then the Reading Room entrance, fish and chip shop and the shoe repairers.

Market Place Shops 1959

EPILOGUE

What better way to end this book than with a quirky fund raiser from the First World War and some epitaphs found in the Old Cemetery.

LIFE, BY A MAN.

MAN comes into this world without his consent and leaves it against his will. On earth he is misjudged and misunderstood. In infancy he is an angel, in boyhood he is a devil, in manhood he is a fool. If he has a wife and family he is a chump, if he is a bachelor he is inhuman. If he enters a public house he is a confirmed drunkard, if he stops out he is a miser. If he is a poor man he has no brains, if he has brains he is considered smart but dishonest. If he goes to Church he is a hypocrite, if he stays away he is a sinful man. If he gives to charity it is for advertisement, if he does not he is stingy and mean. When he comes into the world everyone wants to kiss him, when he goes out everyone wants to kick him. If he dies young there was bound to be a great future for him, if he lives to a ripe old age everybody hopes he has made a will. Life's a funny proposition. There is one thing about life we do know, you can get excellent

Seeds, Nursery Plants and Artificial Manures

from

A. DUCKERING & SONS
EAST BARKWITH, Wragby.

PRICE 3d.
**All Proceeds for Red Cross Agriculture Fund
(Market Rasen effort).**

Of ELIZABETH ROGERSON, 1798 aged 64
> Reader pass on, walk freely o'er my bones
> I lately trod such monumental bones,
> A few days hence shall others tread on thine,
> So small th difference betwixt thy fate and thine.

*****

Of WILLIAM STEPHENSON, 1824 aged 50
> To me 'twas given to die; to thee 'tis given
> to live; alas one moment sets us even,
> Mark how impartial is the till of heaven.

*****

Of ELIZABETH wife of WILLIAM ARDEN, 1818 aged 56
> Life hangs by a slender thread
> No sooner out but we are dead.
> Reader boast not of they might
> We are alive at noon and dead at night.

*****

Of WILLIAM CURTIS, 1856, aged 51
> Why do we mourn dear friends
> Or choke at death's alarms
> 'Tis but the voice that Jesus sent
> To call us to His arms.

*****

Of HENRY CHAMBERS 1869, aged 69
> Life it is a vapour that appeareth
> For a little and then vanisheth away

*****

Finally one that is purported to be in there but hasn't yet been traced.

> Take heed all ye who pass me by
> As you are now, so once was I.
> As I am now, so you will be
> So be prepared to follow me.

In another Churchyard someone had added to the above

> To follow you I'm not content,
> How do I know which way you went.

159